ELC Supervision and Administration

Eileen McPartland

BORU

PRESS

Boru Press Ltd.
The Farmyard
Birdhill
Co. Tipperary
www.borupress.ie

© Eileen McPartland 2022
ISBN 978-1-7396232-2-7

Design by Sarah McCoy
Print origination by Carole Lynch
Index by Eileen O'Neill
Printed by GraphyCems Ltd, Spain

The paper used in this book is made from wood pulp of
managed forests. For every tree felled, at least one tree is planted,
thereby renewing natural resources.

A CIP catalogue record for this book is available from the British Library.
For permission to reproduce photographs and artworks, the author and
publisher gratefully acknowledge the following:

© Shutterstock 6, 11, 21, 27, 41, 48, 50, 58, 64, 93, 95,

The author and publisher have made every effort to trace all copyright
holders, but if any has been inadvertently overlooked we would be
pleased to make the necessary arrangement at the first opportunity.

Boru Press is an independent publisher and is not associated with any
education and training board.

Contents

To Marion O'Brien, Boru Press and their dedicated and ever-present team of miracle workers. Also to my Liberties College students; past, present and future.

Table of figures

Acronyms used in this book

AIM	Access and Inclusion Model
ARP	agenda, record, plan
CAPA	corrective and preventive actions
CBT	cognitive behavioural therapy
CCSP	Community Childcare Subvention Programme
CPD	continuing professional development
CV	curriculum vitae
DCEDIY	Department of Children, Equality, Disability, Inclusion and Youth
DoE	Department of Education
DES	Department of Education and Skills
DJELR	Department of Justice, Equality and Law Reform
ECCE	early childhood care and education
ECEC	early childhood education and care
EI/EQ	emotional intelligence
ELC	early learning and care
EU	European Union
EYEI	Early Years Education Inspection
FFM	five-factor model (of personality)
GDPR	General Data Protection Regulation
GNVB	Garda National Vetting Bureau
ICT	information and communications technology

IQ	intelligence quotient
IT	information technology
LINC	Leadership for Inclusion
MSCEIT	Mayer-Salavey-Caruso Emotional Intelligence Test
NCCA	National Council for Curriculum and Assessment
NSAI	National Standards Authority of Ireland
NSC	National Childcare Scheme
NMW	national minimum wage
OECD	Organisation for Economic Co-operation and Development
QRF	Quality and Regulatory Framework
QQI	Quality and Qualifications Ireland
SAC	school-age childcare
UD	Universal Design
UNCRC	United Nations Convention on the Rights of the Child
VO	visiting officer
WRC	Workplace Relations Commission

Supervision in the ELC Profession

Learning Goals

In this chapter, learners will:

* Examine the concept of self-awareness
* Examine some commonly used personality measurement techniques

Introduction

As a student on professional placement in an early learning and care (ELC) setting, one of the first people you will have been introduced to is a supervisor. This is usually your 'go to' person in the setting whose job ensures the smooth day-to-day running of each element of the setting. Here are some aspects of their role:

* Providing a bridge between you and the setting, facilitating, overseeing and supporting your learning. They are the person whose work, attitude and commitment to care in the setting you should want to replicate.

* Liaising and consulting with other staff to ensure that the procedures and practices in the setting run smoothly.

* Creating and maintaining the atmosphere in the setting and ensuring that all stakeholders are aware of their own contribution to that atmosphere.

* Ensuring that all the policies for the setting are understood, correctly interpreted and appropriately applied throughout the setting.

* Making sure that all stakeholders are informed, consulted and included in decisions within the setting.

* Being a good role model in the ELC workplace by providing examples of best practice in the profession.

* Being the 'go to' person for parents/guardians, workers, trainees, students and contractors in the setting.

* Spotting when things are not being done correctly and implementing changes to fix and prevent problems.

* Overseeing the provision and efficient use of resources, including the collective knowledge and skills of everyone in the ELC setting.

* Facilitating you to reach your potential as a professional in the ELC setting; spotting talent, being supportive, nurturing and encouraging.

* Keeping themselves informed about developments in the sector, developing their own potential and in the process paving the way for others to succeed in the ELC professional setting.

While you may feel that you would like to become a supervisor immediately after completing your studies, you should realise that the level of responsibility that goes with the role of a supervisor in an ELC setting requires a level of emotional maturity that may take some years of observation, oversight, reflective practice and capacity-building to achieve. This process is the reason why professional placements (such as those you have already undertaken throughout your learning) focus on the process of supporting you to *grow* into the role of supervisor rather than passing exams, rote learning and 'ticking boxes'. Good supervisors display many attributes that are developed through practice and reflection rather than being learned from textbooks. This is called experiential learning and is the reason why the process of reflection is so powerful as part of your progression in the ELC professional setting. Thus the role of supervisor is one earned by hard work and emotional intelligence. The process of reaching the level of supervisor is hard and the rewards are often more intrinsic than monetary.

The concept of supervision

Supervision has been labelled 'a complex activity that occurs in a variety of settings and has various functions and modes of delivery' (Wierda 2016). Conceptually, then, the role of the supervisor in an ELC setting is a multi-faceted one, as evidenced by the list of competencies outlined in the previous section. Each facet requires specific skills. The ability to satisfy each facet is what makes a good supervisor great; and a great supervisor is what makes each ELC setting an active part in the lives of all who engage with that setting. For you, it is a privilege to work and learn with a great supervisor and you should endeavour to learn as much as you can so that the skills and competencies you see in your professional placement are ones you can bring with you into your professional ELC career and use to enhance the lives of the children in your care now and into their future.

The layout of this textbook will approach each facet above so that at the end you will understand exactly what the work entails and will be able to emulate those who work with you in your learning journey in the ELC profession.

Figure 1.1 The facets of a supervisor's role

This textbook addresses each facet of the supervisor's role; the skills, competencies, approaches and responsibilities that are part of supervision in an ELC setting; and the required learning that makes a good supervisor.

* **Section 1** examines elements of the self and how knowing and accepting who you are can assist you in your job as a supervisor in an ELC setting.

* **Section 2** explores the concept of professional practice and what is involved in the work of a supervisor, both in a working with and overseeing staff supervisory capacity and a supervisor/supervisee capacity within ELC and the specific challenges this duality can bring.

* **Section 3** will examine the responsibilities of the supervisor for the administration, management, provision and oversight of resources within an ELC setting.

* **Section 4** examines the supervisor's relationships with all stakeholders in an ELC and in particular the relationships with children and with parents/guardians.

Section 1

Self

The Concept of 'Self' in Supervision

Self-awareness

The job of the supervisor in an ELC setting involves a leadership role. One of the fundamental characteristics of a supervisor is being self-aware (George *et al.* 2007), which means that you must understand what you are like, how you operate, what values you have, the attitudes you portray and how each of these attributes affects those around you.

The reason self-awareness is important in the process of development as a supervisor (and even further – as a manager or beyond) is that at each level we work at, we learn how to approach the challenges we encounter so that the job we are focused on gets done. There are always different intensities of challenge that come with each level of a work hierarchy. At each level the person needs to have the expertise, confidence and awareness to be able to analyse the situation, assess the needs required and then  to put an appropriate process in place, while having the courage to face issues that may arise if the action does not resolve the issue.

Self-awareness enables an individual to recognise the reasoning behind the actions they take, to be able to challenge their own beliefs, attitudes and biases and to reflect on the actions already taken (reflection *on* action) or in the process of being taken (reflection *in* action), how those actions were initiated, and to assess the consequences of those actions. It is about a power within you that comes from knowing your own reasoning and the actions you are likely to take, and being able to understand when your actions do not have the desired effect. In this respect the power of self-awareness is seen in the ability of a supervisor taking responsibility for the work of the ELC setting.

Self-awareness is also about knowing your own personality and it can help you to be aware of and recognise personality traits in people who work with you. Knowing and accepting yourself enables you to understand what you can, must or may do in any given situation, it helps you to understand yourself rather than merely criticise yourself internally in response to a difficult situation. It can be very useful in fostering and promoting the development of those you are supervising. The self-awareness of a supervisor is a powerful influence on the smooth running of an ELC setting.

Personality

Personality can be defined as the seemingly invisible characteristics a person has that influence how they deal with daily life. Dignam's (1990) Five-Factor Model of Personality (FFM) looks at five aspects of a person's characteristic behaviours and how they determine what type of personality a person can be classed under. The five factors are:

* Extroversion
* Openness to experience
* Conscientiousness
* Agreeableness
* Emotional stability.

Everyone will have a certain degree of each of these aspects, and according to the FFM the degree of each of these factors in a person's personality can be an indication of how they might react in different situations. Knowing the degree of each factor can assist in the analysis of why people react in particular ways to things they encounter. It is the combination of these factors which allows us to categorise a person's personality type.

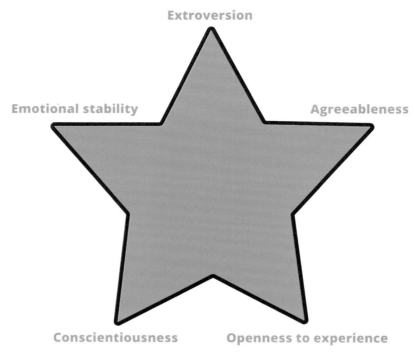

Figure 2.1 The Five-Factor Model of Personality

EXTROVERSION

Many of us know people we think of as extroverts – the people who are outgoing, chatty, comfortable with others and often not afraid to stand out from the crowd. An extrovert may be a very confident person who is not afraid to take on a challenge.

Often extroverts and introverts are described as being polar opposites of each other – introverts being meek and afraid to stand out – and the idea is that you are either one or the other. The reality, however, is that extroversion is a sliding scale; being described as introverted may mean that you do not have an unlimited capacity for extroversion. It is important to understand that you may have different levels of extroversion in different situations. This is particularly the case in relation to taking responsibility and providing support to others, which is fundamental to your leadership or supervision style in an ELC setting.

OPENNESS TO EXPERIENCE

This element of personality relates to a person's openness to embracing new ideas, challenges, ways of looking at the familiar, adaptability and curiosity. This dimension of personality can facilitate seeking solutions when things need to change and finding information about the possibility of change. People who are open to experience are not necessarily always trying new things or doing different jobs; often it is an approach that questions how and why things are done in a specific way and being open to consider how results might change or improve by trying new approaches and adaptations to current processes.

Openness to experience is about deeply reflecting about and upon activities and outcomes and being open to challenges that may present in that process. It is not necessarily about creativity, but the process of questioning procedures and outcomes can result in creativity.

CONSCIENTIOUSNESS

This element of the FFM relates to what people perceive as being responsible, answerable, dependable and focused in our approach to work, life and challenges. It can explain how business people, for instance, can focus on the 'bigger picture' when things get tough and not let events distract them from what needs to be done.

Conscientiousness can be confused with being rigid in decision-making and approach but is probably best explained as a way of focusing on what needs to be done and doing it rather than chopping and changing approaches, which may be wasteful of energy, resources, time or opportunities.

AGREEABLENESS

This refers to the way a person considers the needs and feelings of others in the way they approach challenging situations. It can easily be seen in people who put others first, but there are degrees of agreeableness. A person can consider others but still do what needs to be done in a business-like way. Trust may be easy to establish with an agreeable person and this can help an agreeable person get things done. However, overt agreeableness can lead to the person being perceived as a 'pushover', which can be detrimental to this person as their needs may be overlooked because their agreeableness may be perceived as a lack of confidence or assertion. A balance is important.

EMOTIONAL STABILITY

This refers to a person's ability to handle stress, challenges, criticism and even praise. An emotionally stable person comes across as secure in their position, not threatened by change or perceived competition, and can develop support and encourage positive relationships with others. Once again, emotional stability is a continuum rather than a fixed quantity.

As a group, discuss the five distinct aspects of the FFM and list three strengths and three challenges of each element of the model.

	Strengths		Challenges	
Extroversion	1		1	
	2		2	
	3		3	
Openness to experience	1		1	
	2		2	
	3		3	
Conscientiousness	1		1	
	2		2	
	3		3	
Agreeableness	1		1	
	2		2	
	3		3	
Emotional stability	1		1	
	2		2	
	3		3	

Alternative Personality Measurement Methods

While the FFM is a useful depiction of the elements of personality, several other methods of assessing the concept of self and personality have also been developed.

QUESTIONNAIRES

Personality questionnaires can be useful as a thinking tool and they have become more sophisticated over time. They can be very good at asking you to consider some really pertinent questions in relation to specific events and challenges and how you feel about them, which does get you to think deeply about what matters to you and what you are comfortable dealing with. The format of these questionnaires is usually a range of questions to which you answer yes or no, with a different number of points allocated to each answer. The points scored in the total is then often used as a form of ordering that is then deemed to be indicative of some particular personality.

Questionnaires are often used for online job applications. They can help the potential employer (who usually draws up the questionnaire) to quickly shortlist candidates for interview, but it is important to caution that such questionnaires are usually specifically created and the creator may have skewed the questions in a particular way to get the information they require. In such circumstances they may not help you to get a specific indication of your personality. They are just a record of what you feel or think at a specific moment in time about the scenarios presented in the questions.

Knowing yourself is a process of reflecting on you, your strengths, weaknesses, the things that influence how you act or react, and the things that matter to you. Since these concepts are an evolutionary process, taking a 'reading' of them at a specific point in time will not always give you a final analysis of your individual 'self'. This is also one of the reasons why the process of reflection in ELC is so important; it adds to your skills and competencies and lets you observe over time how you are developing and growing as a person and a professional ELC practitioner through the experiences you encounter.

THE MYERS–BRIGGS TYPE INDICATOR (MBTI™)

The Myers-Briggs Type Indicator is a specific copyrighted tool that was developed and is still owned by the Myers-Briggs Company, which controls its use through franchise arrangements (where people pay a fee to the company in order to use the tool). This process ensures that only licensed operators can use the tool and the Myers-Briggs Foundation receives a payment every time the tool is used. Promotion and advertising of the MBTI™ is controlled by the Myers-Briggs Foundation.

The tool is founded on the writing of Carl Jung, who suggested that personality types could be grouped using four categorisations which are logically connected and can be understood in a format that is easy to group. The Myers-Briggs system was developed by Katharine Cook Briggs and her daughter Isabel Briggs Myers and was loosely based on Carl Jung's work in the 1940's. It was originally aimed at women on the premise that if women could identify their own individual personality preferences they might be able to identify jobs that they were suited to.

The concept used questionnaires of a specific type which were understood to identify personality preferences. These questionnaires have evolved into what is now known as the Myers-Briggs Indicator. It uses a series of forced choice questions; the person doing the questionnaire must choose only one of two possible answers to each question – effectively using opposites as the two choices.

In the MBTI™ the categorisation of personality that emerges is based on four distinct pairs of attitudes which in analysis have the potential to produce 16 different personality types.

The system uses:

* Introversion (**I**) versus Extroversion (**E**)

* Sensing (**S**) versus Intuition (**N**)

* Thinking (**T**) versus Feeling (**F**)

* Judging (**J**) versus Perceiving (**P**).

The final combination of your classified answers then produces a four-letter classification of you of which there are 16 possibilities:

ISTJ	ISFJ	ISFP	ISTP
INTJ	INFJ	INFP	INTP
ESTJ	ESFJ	ESFP	ESTP
ENTJ	ENFJ	ENFP	ENTP

Figure 2.2 The Myers-Briggs personality classifications

Once again the thing to remember about using this tool is that the classification of your personality is based on where you have developed to at the specific point in life. As life itself and your individual experiences may change your reactions or the choices you make, you should remember that, particularly because the MBTI™ uses an either/or procedure, the classification you receive may change over your lifetime.

Employers often use this process to help them select what they identify as the best personality combination for a specific job based on their subjective analysis of the personality type they find best suited to that job. Even in that process the employer themselves may have their own analysis wrong or the correct combination suitable may change with the nature of the job as it evolves.

PSYCHOMETRIC TESTS

A psychometric test (usually but not always administered online) consists of a questionnaire that is used by prospective employers to assess a person's suitability for a particular position and usually uses specific categories to assess the person taking the test.

Psychometric tests normally use categories of test questions based on specific personality competencies and the result can determine whether you are suited to the requirements of the job. The combination is chosen by the employer to test the skills that form part of what they value for the eventual job holder.

Categories can include:

* Verbal reasoning

* Numeric reasoning

* Logic

* Spatial reasoning

* Mechanical ability

* Technical ability

* Concentration and time management

* Error checking.

These tests are not about your overall personality but about the skills you have at that particular time. Participants often realise (usually after the event) that they should have given another answer to a particular question, but these tests are usually time-limited and the anxiety and urgency when answering a long list of questions on different categories of skill can become challenging as time runs out (if you have done your driving theory test you will understand this feeling). That is the plan, however – to see if you are able to do it all within the time.

After a psychometric test, candidates are usually ranked on their final score in the test and chosen for progressing to the next stage of an application process, which saves the employer time interviewing hundreds or thousands of candidates for one or a small number of jobs. In such a scenario it is important to remember that the test is designed for a specific purpose and that your whole personality is not actually assessed (it would be very hard to categorise a winning smile, for instance).

EMOTIONAL INTELLIGENCE

Emotional intelligence (EQ) is sometimes confused with IQ, or intelligence quotient, but it is a very different concept.

As many people understand IQ, it is expressed as a number assigned to a person following a systematic assessment, usually based on verbal, mathematical and logical reasoning. IQ tests quantify how a person scores on specific elements of a combination of tests and questions and this score is classified as your assessment relative to other people, so it can be viewed, and is often interpreted, as a measure of intelligence. Many people who have been assessed as having a low IQ think that they are not intelligent, but they are often highly successful in their chosen careers and may often achieve more than people with higher IQ scores. This has intrigued many researchers over many years.

Howard Gardner looked at this concept in the 1980s and developed a list of intelligences which are still being developed and discussed to this day (Gardner 1983).

The concept of emotional intelligence (EQ) was first popularised by David Goleman (1995). He has continued to write on the topic and a whole industry has grown around the concept. In fact, research into EQ predates Goleman's work; it originated with Peter Salovey and John Mayer, who examined the concept in 1990. The principle of EQ is 'the ability to engage in sophisticated information processing about one's own and others' emotions and the ability to use that information as a guide to thinking and behaviour' (Mayer *et al.* 2008). In the ELC sector, having a high IQ is not necessarily an indicator of success, but a person with a high EQ – who may or may not excel in exams – can be excellent in the ELC sector because they understand their own emotions and those of others, including the children, in particular, and they are able to deal with the emotional challenges that are part and parcel of the ELC sector.

Salovey and Mayer developed their own Four-Branch Model of Emotional Intelligence, which is still used today and has become the basis of what is called the Mayer-Salovey-Caruso Emotional Intelligence Test (MSCEIT) measurement or scoring system. The MSCEIT system consists of eight tasks, two for each of the four branches of the Four-Branch Model (see Figure 2.3) which may consist of recognising emotions in pictures as well as answering questions on aspects of an emotion. The answers are then scored against a pre-determined correct answer.

There is a hierarchical element in the Four-Branch Model developed by Mayer and Salovey: the initial level of EQ (perceiving emotions accurately in oneself and others) is the lowest one in the model; and people with more developed levels of EQ may reach the higher level (managing emotions so as to attain specific goals). Higher-EQ individuals 'are better able to recognise and reason about the emotional consequences of events' (Mayer *et al.* 2008). Once again it is important to note that EQ is a sliding scale, so a person's EQ can change depending on their experiences and what they learn from those experiences.

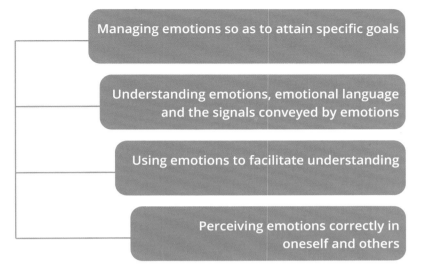

Figure 2.3 The Four-Branch Model of Emotional Intelligence (Mayer & Salovey 1997)

YOUR ETHICS

Job descriptions often include a list of qualities or values the employer seeks in prospective employees. This often includes 'high ethical values'. Ethics is the set of principles you have which directs your behaviour to doing the 'right thing' in a moral dilemma. Being ethical means being conscious of what you should do and ensuring that you do that even if there is an easier choice.

Often the element which challenges your ethics in situations are personal issues that arise and it is very important to remember that when you are employed in an ELC setting you are there to represent, support and care for all the children in your care. You are legally bound to do the right thing for each of those children and that responsibility is particularly important because of the vulnerable nature of those children. There is an internal honesty to being ethical and that is also important when you are in a professional placement with a working supervision relationship. Being honest about your experiences so that they can become part of the supervision conversations you have can help you grow your own ethical position. It is about an inner strength of purpose, sense of responsibility and cultivating strength of character which will stand to you as you work towards becoming a supervisor yourself.

The upside of being ethical is that other people can rely on you to always do what is right and proper. In an ELC setting, where children of all ages need protection and security, being ethical ensures that people feel confident that you will always do what is required by the standards and regulations in ELC.

Go to YouTube and search for 'Developing Emotional Intelligence'.
Now watch the YouTube clip 'Self Awareness – Know Yourself'.

Summary

Throughout the different processes outlined above, which are often used to analyse how your personality can affect the way you work in any given job/situation, it is very important to realise that we constantly learn and develop throughout our lifetime and the concepts we hold about our own abilities and processes can be honed by the challenges we meet on the journey.

It is therefore important to remember that what we think is our 'self' is actually a work in progress and the processes above are a 'snapshot' at a particular time. For example, somebody may initially not be great at supervision because they are reticent about leading the way, for instance, but they could well become much better with practice, challenge, training or situational experience and specific oversight and development on the job. This is why the process of supervision in ELC is such a valuable tool in your own personal career development and it is why supervision can add so much to the staff who work in an ELC setting – and ultimately to the lives and experiences of the children in that setting, their parents/guardians and all stakeholders.

Figure 2.4 Knowing your 'self' puts you at the centre of your learning journey

The processes of setting and overseeing the supervision of professional placement students will be further examined in Section 2.

Recap

1. What are the five factors of personality outlined by Dignam in the FFM?

2. What is the difference between reflection *on* action and reflection *in* action?

3. Explain what the initials I, E, S, N, T, F, J and P stand for in the Myers–Briggs Type Indicator.

4. What do questionnaires, psychometric tests and the Myers–Briggs Type Indicator system have in common?

5. What are the four branches of emotional intelligence outlined by Mayer and Salovey (1997)?

References and further reading

Dignam, J. (1990) 'Personality structure: Emergence of the Five-Factor Model', *Annual Review of Psychology* 41: 417–40

Gardner, H. (1983) *Frames of Mind: The Theory of Multiple Intelligences*. New York: Basic Books

George, W., Sims, P., MacLean, A. and Mayer, D. (2007) 'Discovering your authentic leadership', *Harvard Business Review* 85(2): 129–38

Goleman, D. (1995) *Emotional Intelligence*. New York: Bantam

Mayer, J., Salovey, P. and Caruso, D. (2008) 'Emotional intelligence: New ability or eclectic traits?', *American Psychologist* 63(6): 503–17

Salovey P. and Mayer, J. (1990) 'Emotional intelligence', *Imagination, Cognition and Personality* 9: 185–211

Wierda, K. (2016) 'Exploring interpersonal variables within the supervisory relationship: The role of supervisory alliance, supervisory style and supervisee attachment', doctoral thesis (unpublished), Western Michigan University

Section 2

Professional Practice

3

Supervision and Professional Practice: The Fundamentals

Learning Goals

In this chapter, learners will:

* Learn the definition of supervision in ELC

* Examine the principles of supervision

* Look at the benefits of introducing supervision in ELC settings

Introduction

As outlined in Chapter 2, the role of a supervisor in an ELC setting has a dual aspect.

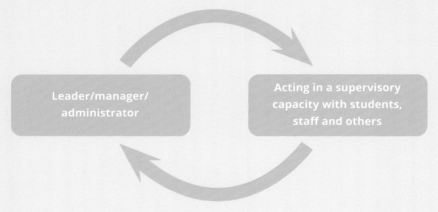

Figure 3.1 The duality of a supervisor's role

The duality arises because the role of supervisor as leader/manager/administrator is the foundation on which a good supervisory relationship will thrive. To be effective the supervisor/supervisee relationship or the supervisory role should be based on the concepts and processes involved in achieving 'best practice'. Best practice should be in place before it can be used as a teaching tool. Thus the core of the duality is the difference between the supervisor as administrator of the setting and the supervisor as teacher/mentor/coach of newly emerging ELC practitioners. Each part of the role feeds the other.

The supervisor as leader/manager/administrator ensures efficiency, regulatory compliance and successful creation and maintenance of an ELC setting in which governance and accountability are paramount in creating a safe, secure, supportive and happy setting in which children thrive. This aspect of the work of the supervisor is the focus of Chapter 4 where the 'setting' element of the facets of a supervisor's job is explored.

In this chapter we will focus on the supervisor in the role of expert assisting the development of the skills, competencies and professional approaches of the students and staff through a supportive educational approach that is grounded in professional reflective practice.

The supervisor's support role

The purpose of supervisory support in an ELC setting is to establish, support and develop good work practices in the setting. It is fundamental to the professional development of those being supervised and it is powerful in establishing models of best practice in reflective practice. Supervision in this context is about establishing trust, support and developmental encouragement for those starting in the ELC setting and providing them with safe processes of interaction with their supervisor in which there is mutual recognition and interaction based on what are considered professional values in that setting.

Supervision is therefore very much a trust-and-respect-based experience involving learning from everyday occurrences, and sense-making of complex learning opportunities in the setting in which the supervision takes place. The most important thing about effective supervision is that it must be a two-way process, and that is why you must understand your own self, as outlined in Chapter 2. Supervision done professionally and with openness is very powerful as it allows for structured learning where the supervisee can make sense of their experiences, can grow and develop their confidence and abilities. This enables them to become strong, effective and eventually able to work independently, at which stage they may be ready to become supervisors themselves. Growing talent from within is also a very significant outcome of the process of supervision.

Before engaging with the process of supervision in your professional placement it is useful to examine the basis on which supervision is grounded.

Defining supervision

Almost every introduction to the concept of supervision will quote Tony Morrison, who described supervision as 'a process by which one worker is given responsibility by the organization to work with another in order to meet certain organizational professional and personal objectives which together promote the best outcomes for service users' (Morrison 2005).

There is a clear sense of a one-way level of responsibility in this definition, but it appears to overlook the fact that supervision is very much a two-way process. The definition used by Southwark Council outlines that 'supervision is a work-focused discussion and/or activity that should provide structure and feedback on day-to-day work, improving practice by critical reflection and fostering an inquisitive approach to work with children and families' (Southwark Council 2015).

Perhaps an even more succinct definition is that supervision is: 'what happens when people who work in the helping professions make a formal arrangement to think with another or others about their work with a view to providing the best possible service to clients, and enhancing their own professional development' (Scaife 2009).

Supervision has become a fundamental process of mutual targeted, timetabled professional discussion and supportive oversight, both *in* practice and *on* practice, that supports the development of competent professional and informed working practices in ELC settings. It is, or certainly should be, in every setting a formal process that adds to the experience of everybody involved.

Principles of supervision

As already outlined, supervision is fundamentally a two-way process. The principles on which it is based are the power tools to ensure its effectiveness:

* The process is based on mutual trust and the ability to be open with each other.
* The supervisor is an advocate for the student in the supervisor/supervisee relationship.

* It provides supports for the education and learning capacity and style of the supervisee while fostering professional conversations on practice. As such, it is intended to deepen the existing understanding and knowledge of the supervisee.

* It ensures a commitment to learning from all involved in a setting – those who see good supervision and those who benefit from it.

* It develops confidence, self-awareness, competencies and skills which ultimately benefit children, parents and the setting.

* It enhances observational practices in an ELC setting.

* It establishes and strengthens respectful working relationships in the setting.

* It helps supervisees to become independent thinkers in best practice development in the ELC setting.

* It ensures that staff at every level feel valued and supported.

All involved in supervision should be mindful of the principles outlined above as this will ensure that the process is positive, progressive and professional.

There is a legal requirement under the Child Care Act 1991 (Early Years Services) Regulations 2016 that every setting has a written policy around supervision in the setting (see page 167) and this requirement enhances the focus on ensuring that every setting follows the principles outlined above.

The benefits of professional supervision in ELC

Supervision in ELC settings has benefits for:

* The ELC setting itself

* The supervisor as leader/manager/administrator

* The supervisee

* The children and other stakeholders.

BENEFITS FOR THE ELC SETTING

* Promotes compliance with regulations, policies and procedures.

* Ensures the quality requirements of the service are fully understood and implemented by all and that all staff realise that they individually have a role to play in the setting's quality framework.

* Develops clear communication channels and co-operative working relationships within the setting between students, staff, supervisors and management.

* Promotes staff development and support structures which assist in staff retention.

* Assists in the development of confident, committed staff who can support the goals of the setting.

* Supports the duty of care responsibilities of the setting.

BENEFITS FOR THE SUPERVISOR AS LEADER/ MANAGER/ADMINISTRATOR

* Improves communication within the setting.

* Allows for the gradual development and sharing of responsibility within the setting.

* Supports the development of competent, informed and thoughtful teams and team members.

* Allows for reflection and the grounding of employee development in professionally supported reflective practice.

* Can reduce fear, stress and anxiety in early career ELC practitioners.

* Identifies learning and continuing professional development (CPD) requirements in the setting.

* It can be a very positive experience to observe how new supervisees view the setting and whether there are areas for improvement in the procedures and practices that might be familiar to the supervisor but are seen differently through fresh eyes.

* Supports deep thinking in the team about their roles, needs and skills.

* Gives the supervisor a bird's eye view of how effective the practices of the setting are, and what might need adjustment.

BENEFITS FOR THE SUPERVISEE

* Gives opportunities to discuss the reasoning behind the practices in the setting.

* Allows for meaningful emphasis on practice during learning.

* Develops confidence and the ability to question how things are done and why.

* Provides support when mistakes are made and the opportunity to learn how to avoid mistakes in the future.

* Offers the possibility to learn outside the classroom in a practical hands-on manner, with support.

* Helps the supervisee to learn to question and to develop an understanding of why things are done in a particular way and of the ethics of ELC environments.

* Helps the supervisee to learn to assimilate learning into practice with support and understanding of the challenges you may face in that process.

* Helps the supervisee to learn how to have professional discussions.

* The supervisee is included in the thinking and processes in the setting and is able to voice opinions and have them considered, which develops agency in the work environment.

BENEFITS FOR CHILDREN AND OTHER STAKEHOLDERS

* Consistency of care and understanding of procedures helps parents/guardians to feel confident about the care and support their own children receive.

* Happy work environments allow staff to thrive and sustain meaningful relationships.

* The development of professional ELC practitioners benefits everyone.

* Reduces potential staff turnover which allows for sustained care standards in an ELC setting.

* Reduces strife, tension and fear in the workplace.

* Creates a collaborative atmosphere for all stakeholders.

Recap

1. **Under what exact Regulation is it a requirement for every ELC setting to have a supervision policy?**

2. **Name two benefits of supervision for:**

   a) **The ELC setting**

   b) **The supervisor as leader/manager/administrator**

   c) **The supervisee in the ELC setting**

   d) **The children in the ELC setting.**

References and further reading

Barnardos (2020) *Supervision and Support in Early Learning and Care*. Dublin: Barnardos

Morrison, T. (2005) *Staff Supervision in Social Care.* Brighton: Pavilion

Scaife, J. (2009) 'Supervision and Personal Development' in J. Hughes and S. Youngson (eds), *Personal Development and Clinical Psychology*, pp. 89–107. British Psychological Society: Wiley-Blackwell

Southwark Council (2015) *London Child Protection Procedures Manual*. London: Southwark Council

4

Supervision and Professional Practice: The Models

Introduction

The way the process of supervision is approached in practice is described as a model of supervision. Each model has specific elements that direct what happens in the process, and the model chosen determines how it happens and why it happens in the way it does. Barnardos (2020) explains that much of what we understand about supervision in ELC is based on practices and approaches that originated in other care settings. Those traditional and formative settings for model-defining approaches included professions such as counselling, psychiatry and psychology where elements of therapy were involved.

Models and theories of supervision

Because therapy, counselling, psychiatry and psychology involve so many different approaches to treatment there are just as many variations of supervision that are appropriate to the types of treatment. Each methodology brings its own type of emphasis on the supervisor/supervisee relationship. There are therefore varied structures of supervision models, and some of those models are very alike, with only subtle differences of approach.

These models include:

* Directive model

* Collaborative model

* Alternative supervision

* Non-directive model

* Process model (Hawkins & Shohet 2012) – also called the 7 Eyes Model

* Discrimination model (Bernard & Goodyear 2004)

* Functions model (Kadushin 2002)

* Cognitive behaviour model

* Psychotherapy-based model.

This textbook will not cover all these models since some of them are more relevant to the context of the therapy processes they are used in and are not transferable to the processes and structures of an ELC setting. What is important to realise, however, is that they are all founded on a process of reflective practice that facilitates the review of actions, feelings, challenges and achievements about which the supervisee is facilitated to feel confident to discuss and receive direction on. Whatever system of reflection you practice (e.g. Schön (1983), Kolb (1984), Gibbs (1988) and even the three-question What, So What, Now What process (Rolfe *et al.* 2001)) there is a step element to the process of reflection. It is imperative that the supervisee has, within the supervision process, gone through those steps themselves and understands, through the steps, what it is they are looking at, questioning or seeking to tease out understanding about.

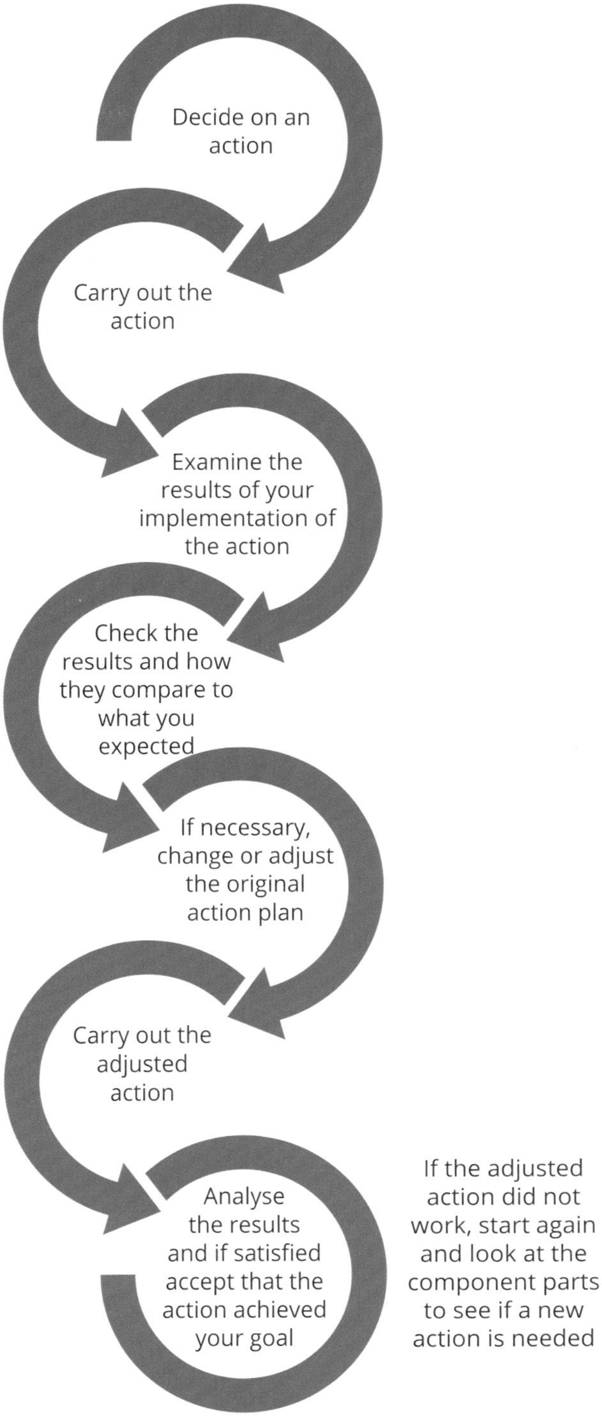

Decide on an action

Carry out the action

Examine the results of your implementation of the action

Check the results and how they compare to what you expected

If necessary, change or adjust the original action plan

Carry out the adjusted action

Analyse the results and if satisfied accept that the action achieved your goal

If the adjusted action did not work, start again and look at the component parts to see if a new action is needed

Figure 4.1 A generic model of reflection (adapted from Kolb (1984), Gibbs (1988), Schön (1983) and Rolfe et al. (2001))

The supervision process that any supervisor embraces is based on their own experience and the relational basis on which they work with others. There is no right or wrong model in any specific setting as long as it reflects the individual elements of the setting (e.g. therapy vs. business, etc.). Professional conversations that happen in supervision sessions should be based on effective reflection on the elements of that professional conversation so that the supervision session adds to a supervisee's developmental learning. Here we will examine a small number of models that help to illustrate the different approaches to supervision and how the process works.

Inskipp and Proctor (1995a, 1995b) observe that there are different tasks within any specific model of supervision which are negotiated (described as a 'working alliance') between the supervisor and supervisee as the process of supervision develops:

* **Formative** – the supervisee's skills development, learning and professional journey

* **Normative** – the concepts of best practice, accountability and compliance requirements

* **Restorative** – the impact of the work and the psychological supports that build esteem.

Both the supervisor and the supervisee must ensure that the process of supervision they are engaged in works, and they both have a part to play in making it work effectively.

THE DISTRIBUTIVE MODEL OF SUPERVISION

This model is aligned to the concept of distributed leadership and suggests that supervision should be diffused as much as possible within an organisation (Watson 2002). It is based on the notion that best learning within an organisation does not necessarily come from just one person but that organisations that use supervision have different experts or specialists at different levels or in different departments in the organisation; supervision is best carried out by a range of supervisors and the supervisee can learn different aspects from each specialist.

Brigid Proctor (1987) identified issues of joint responsibility that underpin this model. She outlined that there are three distinct tasks of supervision:

1. **Normative** – taking responsibility for standards and ethics

2. **Formative** – sharing responsibility for the development of the supervisee in skills, knowledge and understanding

3. **Restorative** – providing opportunities for discharge and recharge of the supervisee's skills and knowledge.

In ELC settings in Ireland, children are usually divided into room groups based on the child:carer ratios for their age profile (e.g. baby, toddler, etc., with different supervisors in each room). This does not necessarily lend itself to effective application of a distributive model of supervision except where staff/learners are given time with different age groups and different supervisors. If this were the case, different styles of supervision might apply in each area of specialism; while this is not necessarily a problem it is a possible feature (Ebbeck & Waniganayake 2003). Additionally, there might be boundary issues in relation to access to particular supervisors and navigating the boundaries could challenge learners, particularly at the initial learning stage (Hayden 1996).

THE DEVELOPMENTAL MODEL OF SUPERVISION

This model acknowledges that people's experience, confidence and skills develop over time and are not fixed at a specific point in time. Despite this the skilled supervisor can often identify what skills the supervisee needs to develop and can advise, oversee and support them to do so.

The developmental model also identifies that the supportive elements or intensity of supervision needs to change as the supervisee becomes more capable, confident and professionally aware of their role in an organisation where 'the path towards proficiency is developmental' (Stoltenberg 2005, p. 858). Stoltenberg suggested that the focus is different depending on the level the supervisee has reached, and he identified three levels of supervisees:

* **Beginner** – the focus in on skill acquisition, there is a high level of anxiety and the motivation to learn is high.

* **Intermediate** – the motivation wavers as the level of complexity of tasks increase and this can lead to wobbles in confidence.

* **Advanced** – levels of motivation have stabilised and temporary doubts are not as disabling. The supervisee has moved towards a professional identity stage where they understand the need to continue to learn and will do so as part of a lifelong learning continuum.

Following on from these three stages of development, in the development model of supervision there is a corresponding decrease in the intensity of the supervision process as the supervisee develops (Stoltenberg & Delworth 1987).

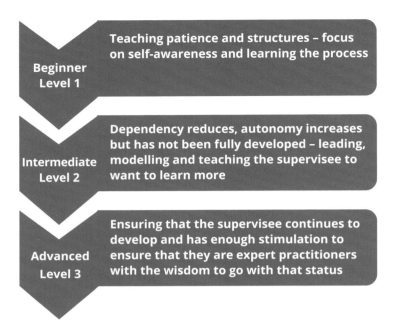

Figure 4.2 Focus of supervision in the development model

Learn more to develop your understanding

Design a poster that demonstrates the levels of intensity a supervisee needs during the process of supervision in a way that makes it easy for you to understand and remember.

If you do find this idea difficult to understand, think about how your own learning has developed through your educational journey and what elements of support you now know would have been helpful when you started out on your journey. Design a poster to show what you mean.

THE PROCESS MODEL OF SUPERVISION

The process model has been described as one that lends itself specifically to the caring professions (Hawkins & Shohet (2012), which relates specifically to a therapy scenario). It introduced the concept of 'modes' where the process of supervision differs in each mode and is clearly outlining a process that takes place over an extended period of time. The seven modes of the Process Model are:

* Mode 1 Content of the Supervision Session

* Mode 2 Strategies and Interventions

* Mode 3 Therapy relationship

* Mode 4 Therapist's processes

* Mode 5 Supervisory relationship

* Mode 6 Supervisor's own process

* Mode 7 Wider context (expanding outside the session).

As with many of the models, the process is directed by the overall aim of and contexts in which the model is used. This specific approach does not easily fit into an ELC framework as ELC does not have a therapy element. It is useful, however, to examine models such as this for their insight that the supervision process has component parts and that there are elements which expand as the understanding of the process develops.

THE REFLECTIVE LEARNING MODEL OF SUPERVISION

As already mentioned, reflection is a major part in the learning processes in ELC settings. Different approaches to reflection have been explored by writers such as Kolb (1984), Gibbs (1988) and Schön (1983). Once you are familiar with the reflection process you will understand the concept of the reflective learning model of supervision, which facilitates both supervisor and supervisee to:

* Explore a supervisee's practice and factors influencing their practice responses (including emotions, assumptions, power relations and the wider social context)

* Develop a shared understanding of the knowledge base informing their analysis and the limitations of their thinking, and

* Uses this understanding to inform next steps. (Wonnacott 2012)

You will have already grasped that the reflective learning model is effective in ELC settings because of the embedded practice of reflection, a powerful tool for all practitioners in the ELC sector, which you will have learned in your ELC training.

In the reflective model of supervision:

* Supervision is driven by the experiences of the learner.

* The supervisor ensures that there is space and context for the supervisee to learn.

* The supervisor takes the role of facilitator so that the supervisee learns to accept, understand and own the decisions they make in the process.

* The process of supervision is part of an ongoing learning process that involves andragogical and experiential learning at its heart. (Rush & Shelden 2020)

A further consideration in any approach to reflective models of supervision is the freedom the supervisee should have to question, without fear, the practices in a setting. This demands trusting, confidence-building and supportive structures in the setting where the supervision takes place. Fundamental elements that help support the process are:

* A space in which practitioners can build their capacity to think about and analyse complex situations they see in practice

* Containment for practitioners' emotional response to direct work, such as a debriefing session which respects the feelings of practitioners

* A means for practitioners to make use of their own experience and develop awareness of how their experience informs their practice. (Morrison 2001; Sheppard 1998)

The understanding that needs to be established in a reflective model of supervision is succinctly explained by Ruch, who outlined four specific levels of reflection that lead to deeper reflection; supervisors can decide which to focus on or can use all the levels to support the supervision process:

* **Technical** – compares the actual performance of the supervisee with what it is right to do in the setting. There is a concentration on policies, procedures and centre practices.

* **Practical** – looks back at what experience has taken place and encourages the supervisee to reflect both *in* action (actions, feelings, decision-making and focus on results of actions taken) and *on* action (theoretical reasons why things are done a specific way and how that impacts on the supervisee, their practices and understanding).

* **Critical** – allows and encourages assessment of self-growth in the process and examines power situations and impacts on the supervisee's concept of self and development.

* **Process** – looks at how the work involved impacts on the judgements of the practitioner and their emotional responses to the way things are learned and implemented. It involves a sense of them committing to the structures of their work. (Ruch, 2000)

MORRISON'S 4X4X4 MODEL OF SUPERVISION

This model is seen as the most applicable to ELC settings and is the model most often applied in Ireland (Barnardos 2020). This is a specifically 'integrated' model of supervision which consists of three cycles of four elements each. The three cycles outlined by Gibbs *et al.* (2014) operate as a multi-dimensional model.

A. **The outer four** relate to the four functions of supervision:

1. **Support** – setting up, getting to know the supervisee and clarifying boundaries between support, counselling and limits on confidentiality which will be the foundation of the process.

2. **Management** – ensuring that the policies and procedures of the setting are understood and that the supervisees know their own responsibilities; recording sessions; ensuring that the supervisee knows when to seek advice and direction.

3. **Development** – assisting the supervisee to set appropriate goals for themselves, to learn how to react to advice and constructive feedback; and to see the bigger picture and the impact of their work on all stakeholders in the ELC setting.

4. **Mediation/organisation** – involving the supervisee in the internal workings of the organisation; they learn to understand their own contribution to the organisation, such as policy and procedure development, and learn about the outside influences of and for the organisation.

B. **The middle four** relate to internal drivers of the supervision process, based on models of reflection such as Gibbs, Kolb or Schön. (Kolb's is sometimes favoured as it incorporates feelings and envisaging the impact of actions in the process of reflection.) Thus the middle four consists of the Kolb's elements:

1. Experience

2. Reflection

3. Analysis

4. Plan and act.

You will have learned this aspect of the 4x4x4 model in your earlier studies of the ELC professional training and your place in it.

C. **The inner four** relate to the four main stakeholders in ELC settings:

1. Children and their families

2. Staff, including the supervisee

3. The ELC setting and its managers/owners

4. External agencies with which the ELC setting engages (e.g. Tusla).

When all three of the four-part cycles are put together it forms a nestled three-cycle 'integrated' 4x4x4 model (with children and stakeholder at the centre). This was outlined by Morrison and is depicted as three clear cycles which indicate the depth of the whole 4x4x4 model of supervision (see Figure 4.3).

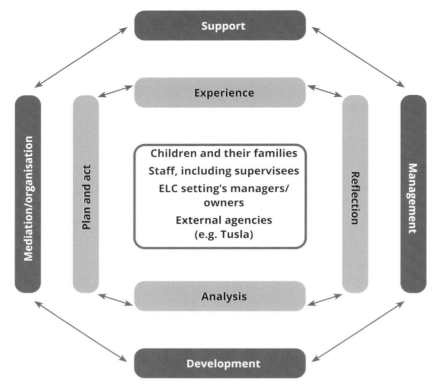

Figure 4.3 4x4x4 model of supervision (Morrison 2005)

Recap

1. **Name the three tasks of supervision outlined by Proctor (1987) and developed by Inskipp and Proctor (1995).**

2. **Outline the three stages of proficiency according to Stoltenberg and Delworth (1987) and explain what they mean for a supervisor.**

3. **Name the elements of Morrison's 4x4x4 model of supervision in each of the following three cycles:**

   a) the inner four

   b) the middle four

   c) the outer four

4. **What is the essential driver of the 4x4x4 model of supervision?**

References and further reading

Barnardos (2020) *Supervision and Support in Early Learning and Care*. Dublin: Barnardos

Bernard, J. and Goodyear, R. (2004) *Fundamentals of Clinical Supervision* (3rd edn). Boston MA: Pearson

Ebbeck, M. and Waniganayake, K. (2003) *Early Childhood Professionals: Leading Today and Tomorrow*. Sydney: Mclennan Petty

Gibbs, G. (1988) *Learning by Doing: A Guide to Teaching and Learning Methods*. Oxford Further Education Unit, Oxford Polytechnic

Gibbs, J., Dwyer, J. and Vivekananda, K. (2014) *Leading Practice: A Resource Guide for Child Protection Leaders*. Melbourne: Victorian Government Department of Human Services, Child Protection

Hawkins, P. and Shohet, R. (2012) *Supervision in the Helping Professions* (4th edn). Maidenhead: Open University

Hayden, J. (1996) *Management of Early Childhood Services: An Australian Perspective*. Sydney: Social Science Press

Inskipp, F. and Proctor, B. (1995a) *The Art, Craft and Tasks of Counselling Part 1: Making the Most of Supervision*. Twickenham: Cascade

Inskipp, F. and Proctor, B. (1995b) *The Art, Craft and Tasks of Counselling Part 2: Becoming a Supervisor*. Twickenham: Cascade

Kadushin, A. (2002) *Supervision in Social Work*. New York: Columbia University Press

Kolb, D. (1984) *Experiential Learning: Experience as a Source of Learning and Development*. Englewood Cliffs NJ: Prentice Hall

Morrison, T. (2001) *Staff Supervision in Social Care: Making a Real Difference for Staff and Service Users*. Brighton: Pavilion

Morrison, T. (2005) *Staff Supervision in Social Care*. Brighton: Pavilion

Proctor, B. (1987) *Supervision: A Co-operative Exercise in Accountability: Enabling and Ensuring: Supervision in Practice*. MM and PM Leicester, National Youth Bureau/ Council for Education and Training in Youth and Community Work

Rolfe, G., Freshwater, D. and Japer, M. (2001) *Critical Reflection in Nursing and the Helping Professions: A User's Guide*. Basingstoke: Palgrave Macmillan

Ruch, G. (2000) 'Self and social work: Towards an integrated model of learning', *Journal of Social Work Practice* 14(2): 99–112

Rush, D. and Shelden, M. (2020) *The Early Childhood Coaching Handbook* (2nd edn). Baltimore MD: Paul H. Brooks Publishing

Schön, D. (1983) *The Reflective Practitioner: How Professionals Think in Action*. New York: Basic Books

Sheppard, M. (1998) 'Practice validity, reflexivity and knowledge for social work', *British Journal of Social Work* 28(5): 763–81

Stoltenberg, C. and Delworth, U. (1987) *Supervising Counsellors and Therapists: A Developmental Approach*. San Francisco CA: Jossey-Bass

Stoltenberg, C. (2005) 'Enhancing professional competence through developmental approaches to supervision', *American Psychologist* 60(8): 857–64

Watson, T. (2002) *Organising and Managing Work: Organisational Managerial and Strategic Behaviour in Theory and Practice*. Harlow: Pearson Education

Wonnacott, J. (2012) *Mastering Social Work Supervision*. London: Jessica Kingsley

5

Supervision and Professional Practice: Putting it All Together

Learning Goals

In this chapter, learners will:

* Learn about the importance of thinking deeply

* Examine the benefits for learning of placements and practicums in ELC settings

* Examine the difference between analysis, hypothesising, critical thinking, intuition and deliberation in reflective practice

* Learn about different models of supervision

* Learn about the regulatory need for a supervision policy

* Examine the elements of supervision procedures

* Delve into the component parts of a supervision policy

* Learn what is involved in setting up a supervision process in an ELC setting

Introduction

In this chapter you will further explore the concept of supervision and the need for proper procedures that serve to locate the process of supervision in the development and support of professional practice in ELC settings. You will learn the value of professional work placements/practicums in your early-stage career development and you will learn how to put a supervision process in place in an ELC setting once you become a supervisor. You will also consider how your own developing skills of reflective practice will prepare you for supervision throughout your career. Recognising how your own reflective and supervision needs are met is a fundamental part of your development as a supervisor.

Professional placements or practicums

At the very beginning of your professional journey in the ELC sector, you are required as part of your learning to undertake a number of professional placements where you can engage and learn in real-life ELC settings. This type of experience serves to embed your theoretical learning in a practical sense in a range of settings in order to contribute to your development as a professional practitioner. Such placements are often referred to as practicums.

A practicum gives students real-life experiences and opportunities outside the classroom that help them put their learning into context. Students see the explanations of what they are learning and how the topics they are learning about in the classroom are put into practice. The process involves practical and conceptual learning on-site (Huggins 2017). You will notice that different settings may have different approaches to issues that arise, for reasons that may relate to, for example, the children, the staff or the setting context. Each practicum setting offers you a rich source of experiential learning and you should approach each as an opportunity for learning that will enrich your expertise as an ELC practitioner.

In a practicum, the experience you get is limited to the time you are given for each practicum in each individual setting. The supervision you experience in those professional placements will be structured by your college in consultation with the practicum setting to ensure that you get the best learning experience specific to you at your point of professional learning development. Your college, specifically your monitor of professional placement, and the supervisor in the practicum setting will collaborate closely to ensure that your learning and professional development needs are maximised for you.

As a student on practicum or professional work placement, you are a very important part of that process too, so you should engage fully with each practicum to maximise your own learning in a way that informs the development of your personal understanding and application of your learning at college. You should view your practicums as a development process and be open to the experiences you have. Being a passive observer is not the same as being an engaged learner and professional contributor to your own professional learning and expertise. Engage in and contribute to the process so that you can get the best from each opportunity to put your learning into practice – that is part of what will make you a competent, expert professional in ELC.

The benefits of learning while on practicum include:

* Supported learning in which your placement monitor and the setting supervisor collaborate with you in your own interest.

* Experiential development of theory and practice in individual settings in a process of sense-making.

* A chance to observe the norms of behaviour and practice in a range of settings.

* Applying the skills you are learning about in a way that makes sense of that learning and seeing how the theories and terminologies you are being taught are applied in practice.

* Developing confidence and competencies in a range of ELC settings.

* Skills development focused on being recognised as a professional practitioner in ELC.

* Opportunities to observe the practices of others in a range of settings.

* The opportunity to expand your CV with references and actual on-the-job experiences.

* Increasing your networking and community of practice experiences while learning the importance of this in your career development.

* Increasing your potential to be considered for permanent employment in an ELC setting.

It's possible that not every practicum you undertake will meet your expectations, but such experiences are also part of your learning. You will realise that there are all levels of practice throughout ELC settings and some will be more relevant than others to

what you want to learn and how you feel your own concept of learning should be applied. This will help you develop your reflective skills so that when you become a full part of an ELC setting you will be well placed to benefit from the supervision we discussed in the last chapter. Just as no two learners are the same, no two ELC placements are the same. Experiencing varied practicums will help make sense of the discussions around the process of supervision within this chapter and enable you to observe those concepts in your practicum in a way that informs your learning. Indeed, it will help you to understand the basis of your practicum agreement and why the concepts and processes in that agreement are stated in the way they are and what the theories behind the concept of practicum mean for you as a developing professional practitioner in ELC, a personal learner and a nascent supervisor who will help others develop to their best potential in an ELC environment in your future career.

Thinking as part of reflective practice and effective supervision

The process of reflection at the heart of Morrison's 4x4x4 model of supervision (Morrison 2005) outlined in the last chapter involves embedding and supporting *effective reflection* in staff members at each stage of their professional journey. This requires that supervisors may need to support supervisees to arrive at a level of professional development where they can think critically about their practice when working or interacting with children, families, staff and others in an ELC setting. This is fundamental to the development of good practitioners and it has been pointed that 'it is the quality of "thinking" that dictates the quality of practice and ultimately, the effectiveness of any support provided to children and their families' (Brown & Turney 2014). For Brown and Turney it is important that the practitioner knows what they think and, more important, they need to question why they think that way.

This type of critical thinking and analysis can be supportively encouraged by a skilful supervisor who can:

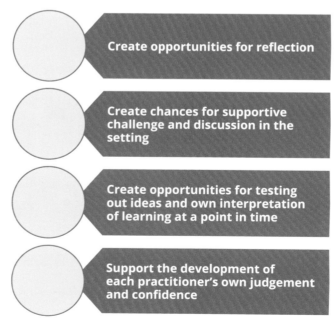

Create opportunities for reflection

Create chances for supportive challenge and discussion in the setting

Create opportunities for testing out ideas and own interpretation of learning at a point in time

Support the development of each practitioner's own judgement and confidence

Figure 5.1 Supervisor skills that contribute to thinking (Brown & Turney 2014)

In their discussions on the process of developing critical thinking in practitioners, Brown and Turney outline a number of different modes of thinking: analysis; hypothesising; critical thinking; intuition; and deliberation.

ANALYSIS

This means looking at the individual parts of a situation and analysing those different parts and how they relate to each other. To envisage this process, think about the difference between a two-dimensional image like a photograph and a three-dimensional image such as a satellite image of the same scene (try looking at a Google Maps image of your own street). The three-dimensional image shows more detail and includes more revealing surrounding images that help make more sense of the two-dimensional picture.

Being open to possibilities, making sense of things and being able to say what you think and why you think that way is at the centre of being able to analyse. This can be achieved by looking at every aspect of the subject matter and considering the different things that make it seem the way it does (e.g. consider if it would or would not seem the same way to somebody else).

HYPOTHESISING

This involves considering different interpretations of facts that are available to you and looking for details that you may have left out of the consideration process. In the process of hypothesising you should consider how the facts appear to you as you see them now, and how they might appear to you if you were to consider another explanation. For example, if a small child did not react to a loud bang that frightened every other child in the room you might hypothesise that they have a hearing difficulty.

CRITICAL THINKING

Look at and consider other options for action to the ones you always choose. Ask yourself 'Why not ...?' Reading and research around your subject may help you develop your critical thinking skills. A good supervisor/supervisee relationship will encourage you to question why something is always done a certain way and why it works. Critical thinking is not about being absolutely certain about something. It is about using sound information and research to increase the likelihood that you can stand over your decision (Taylor & White 2006).

INTUITION

This is about how what you have learned to date in your life can suggest different ways of doing something or looking at something from a different perspective. This could relate to your experience, what you have read around the topic in question, or even what you have seen done somewhere else (e.g. on your practicums).

DELIBERATION

Think about how and why you implement action and how it is considered 'best fit' for the situation you are thinking about. Think about how other options might better fit the detail and decide why you would not choose one specific type of action above another option.

Gibbs extolled the benefit of thinking beyond your experiences when he pointed out that 'without reflection upon this experience it may quickly be forgotten, or its learning potential lost. It is from the feelings and thoughts emerging from this reflection that generalisations or concepts can be generated. And it is ... generalisations that allow new situations to be tackled effectively' (Gibbs 1988, p. 9).

It is useful at this stage to discuss the concept of critical reflection as outlined by Brookfield (1995). Critical reflection requires the learner to consider others in their reflection in what he called 'critical lenses' (Brookfield 1995, p. 31) such as the views of:

* The practitioner themselves (self)

* The children they work with

* The colleagues they work with

* Theories and literature.

You can apply the same process to ensure that your reflection is not one-dimensional. Applying these lenses to your reflection will help you to really understand that there are many ways of understanding something. Using these critical lenses will give you a deeper understanding of what you are learning, seeing and doing in your setting.

THINK AND REFLECT

Ask one of your classmates to suggest a topic for this exercise from their own experiences on placement/practicum (any topic should work).

First, the student outlines what they understand to be the important aspects of the issue they are presenting (self).

Next, divide your class into three groups.

* Group 1 looks at the issue from the point of view of the children in the setting.

* Group 2 looks at the issue from the point of view of other workers in the setting, how they deal with the issue and why they view it that way.

* Group 3 looks at how the literature deals with the issue.

Each group presents and explains their findings.

Finally, the class examines what has changed about their understanding of the issue after they have listened to every group.

One of the most important things to remember in your practicum experience is that you don't just turn up and do what you are told without actually 'thinking' while you do so. That process of thinking is at the heart of critical reflection and is supported by your continued learning, research and a sense of wanting to learn all about the profession you wish to become part of. The more you put into the process the better the outcomes will be and the more you will benefit throughout your professional career in ELC. It is very much a two-way street.

Extend Your Learning

 Read about the processes involved in Munro's Decision Tree (Munro *et al.* 2016) and suggest ways in which they could be interpreted in your practice.

THINK AND REFLECT

1. Explain how knowing and considering the consequences of actions you prepare to take can help you become a competent ELC practitioner.

2. Design a flowchart poster for a process that you regularly undertake in a certain way and include 'What if …?' as part of that flowchart. Discuss what type of thinking is involved in this process.

Models of supervision

It should be obvious from what has been described in relation to supervision in this and the previous chapter that the task of good supervision in an ELC setting can be a rewarding and enabling process that can empower staff and contribute to their professional development while supporting the daily challenges, rewarding experiences and constant individual learning that is so much a part of everyday work in an ELC environment. Done well, supervision informs practice, challenges norms, builds on the mission of the setting and, in so doing, contributes to a feeling of involvement, contribution and support for the children, staff, parents and other stakeholders in ELC settings and, indeed, in other settings where the individual learning of well-trained ELC practitioners is applied.

The challenge for a good supervisor is to ensure that the different levels and intensities of supervision needed at beginner, intermediate and advanced supervisee levels (as outlined by Stoltenberg & Delworth (1987)) are facilitated and balanced with the ongoing work of the setting and the needs of children, staff and all stakeholders. This challenge can be reflected in different models of supervision that can be applied at all or any one of those supervisee levels.

INDIVIDUAL ONE–TO–ONE SUPERVISION

This type of supervision may happen in hierarchical structures. Your managing supervisor may interact with you on an individual basis to discuss and tease out meanings about your approaches, learning and development. It need not be your own individual manager but could be someone who is familiar with the work you have been doing and can add context and substance to the issues you have encountered while facilitating you in reviewing your own contribution in the setting.

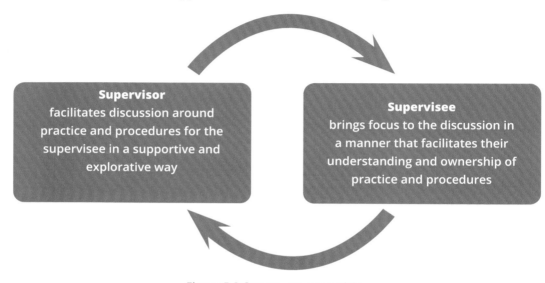

Supervisor
facilitates discussion around practice and procedures for the supervisee in a supportive and explorative way

Supervisee
brings focus to the discussion in a manner that facilitates their understanding and ownership of practice and procedures

Figure 5.2 One-to-one supervision

It is important to bear in mind that the whole process of supervision is not intended to focus on your shortcomings in the setting or on the minute details of your daily work. It should be a process of discussing your progress, your questions around procedures and practices, and it should be focused on facilitating you in your professional development. It will also include positive comments; and perhaps your reasoning may inform the setting's practices where they have seen you do something which was successful in a particular situation. It should not be a top-down approach but a meeting-of-minds approach with development of skills and competencies as preferred outcomes.

Carried out professionally, one-to-one supervision can be powerful and can contribute to a feeling of confidence. Working closely with only one person in the supervision process can allow both the supervisor and the supervisee to build a trusting and supportive relationship. In order for such supervision to work well, there should be clearly outlined structures to the process of supervision. We shall return to this later in this chapter.

GROUP SUPERVISION

Group supervision sessions are run in much the same way as a one-to-one session in relation to the processes involved, but a group session might involve a team of staff discussing something of value to the whole group. A group supervision session could also be a multi-agency meeting involving for example a play therapist, occupational therapist, speech and language therapist and/or other agency group members discussing a particular development in the setting or profession.

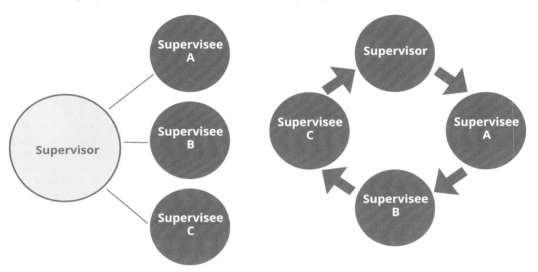

Figure 5.3 Group supervision models

A group supervision session can be a peer session, where everyone contributes as equals, or it can be based on a supervisor and a number of supervisees who are all benefiting from the session, with the supervisor providing advice and guidance for each supervisee equally. Group supervision sessions can be powerful as the interests of a range of professionals can create a very rounded discussion and lead to valuable learning and support for the whole group. In group supervision personal issues and challenges will seldom be the focus; group supervision is more often used for situational discussions on specific topics of interest to the whole group. They might also, for example, involve discussing how to interpret changes that are happening in the sector and how they will impact on work practices for the whole group. They could also be a wraparound examination of issues that have arisen for a specific child.

In group supervision it is important to realise that you are part of a group. You need to listen to what everyone has to say. Ask questions, acknowledge the position everyone is coming from and contribute your own expertise when appropriate, while being sensitive to the contributions of everyone in the group.

Group supervision cannot and should not replace individual supervision; instead, it should enhance it. Each staff member has a right to supervision and it is part of the setting's duty of care to the staff to ensure that they are receiving the correct support in undertaking the duties assigned to them.

AD HOC SUPERVISION

This is supervision that happens in less predictable situations than formally timetabled supervision sessions. It could arise because something happens that needs a discussion immediately or because a conversation leads to a decision or understanding of a new situation and where more discussion will help everyone who might work on

that situation. This can often happen in ELC settings where the unpredictability of children and family issues can call for supported decisions or understanding to take place quickly.

It is important that ad hoc sessions are not considered the norm as that would take away from the benefits of structured supervision. There should be the same level of thought in an ad hoc situation

Ad hoc supervision can happen at any time and place

as in planned supervision – not just a quick answer from a supervisor – to avoid undermining the goal of encouraging a supervisee to develop independent but supported thinking.

COMMUNITIES OF PRACTICE

Communities of practice are similar to peer-led group supervision. The difference is that in a community of practice the supervisees may not actually work in the same setting but may be doing similar jobs in different settings. It may be that all staff in a particular setting who operate at the same level in different rooms in the setting get together to have regular discussions about their practices, developments in the setting, or developments in ELC in general. It could even be the case that the community of practice exists in one setting with all staff contributing to discussions and feedback on issues that arise. The important word is 'community'; participants have similar and shared interests and are willing to support each other collegially as a cohesive learning group in their interactions with each other (Lave & Wenger 1991). A community of practice also includes beginners and more experienced practitioners who develop their own sense of position, belonging and expertise within the community through what Lave and Wenger describe as 'legitimate peripheral participation' (1991, p. 29). They are places where theories and ways of understanding are developed, negotiated and shared (Wenger 1998).

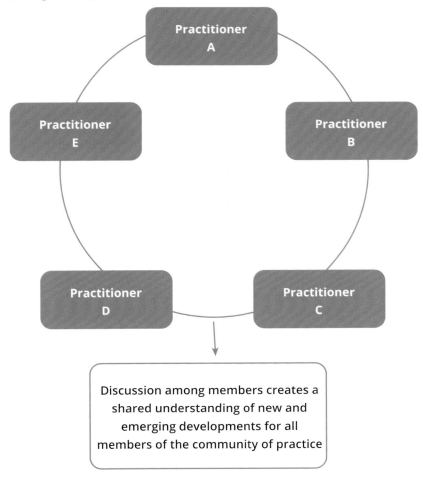

Figure 5.4 A community of practice

The move to more technology-based interactions and meeting platforms such as Zoom or Teams has facilitated a growth of communities of practice – people can meet without being physically in the same place. The rapid pace of change in ELC has led to diverse groups meeting, discussing and disseminating new and emerging ideas in ELC environments.

BUDDY SYSTEMS

In some ELC settings early career practitioners may be 'buddied' with more experienced practitioners who guide the new recruit through the ways in which procedures are understood in that particular setting. This differs slightly from one-to-one supervision as the buddy will not have a procedurally defined role as a supervisor, but they will add to the experience of the newer recruit by ensuring that the correct procedures are understood and applied. This is not about teasing out understanding, meaning or exploring issues; it is about helping a new or emerging member of a team to quickly integrate into the setting.

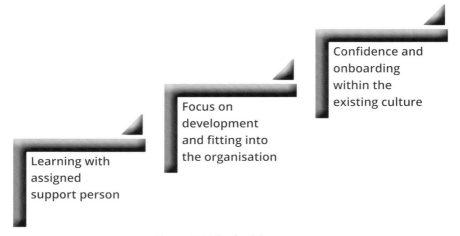

Figure 5.5 The buddy system

A buddy system can be an effective way of inducting new members of a team and helping them establish a feeling of trust and mutual understanding of everyone's role in the setting. It gives them a 'go-to' person for questions that may arise in the initial phase of settling in to a new role. It may also set the scene for establishing a one-to-one supervision relationship once the inductee has settled and has a grasp of what is expected of them. A buddy is likely to be at a

different level of professional development (Stoltenberg & Delworth 1987); for example, an intermediate-level supervisee may be a buddy to a beginner-level supervisee and they will assist each other in a mutual process of development.

Additionally, in line with inclusion processes and equality legislation, a buddy system can enable a staff member with additional needs to fully participate in a setting. Here, the buddy looks out for issues that might arise for the staff member with the additional needs and mediates the challenges or ensures that the setting is all-ability proofed for that staff member. An anti-bias approach in a setting should apply to staff and others, and when it is well done it acts as a best practice role model for everyone in the setting.

MENTORING

Mentoring is a two-person process that can be very enabling. A mentor usually has much more experience than the mentee and is willing to support the mentee to walk their own individual developmental journey. The mentor will not instruct the mentee but will act like a 'sage on the stage' (King 1993); their experience will enable the mentee to explore and question issues they want clarity about.

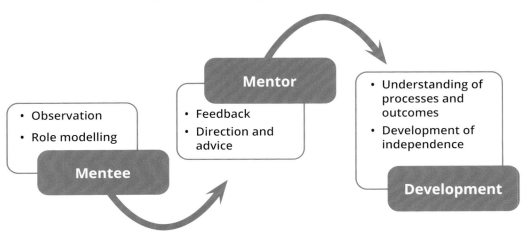

Figure 5.6 Mentoring

Mentors usually take a personal interest in the development of the mentee and support them to understand, plan and execute the best career moves for them. The mentor–mentee relationship differs from the supervisor–supervisee relationship in this particular aspect as the supervisor will not give direct targeted career development guidance but will support the supervisee to become as good as they can at the level they are at. At the heart of mentoring is the sharing of knowledge between the mentor and mentee and the mentee's observation of the mentor's behaviours and ways of working, so that role modelling is part of the process.

COACHING

Coaching means assisting others to improve their performance so that they can be more successful, or 'unlocking a person's potential to maximise their own performance' (Whitmore 2009). The process, while similar to supervision, is more focused on facilitating the individual to become more successful at what they already do, or pointing them in the direction they need to go. In that respect coaching is often seen as a directional process rather than a mutually consultative reflective-based process.

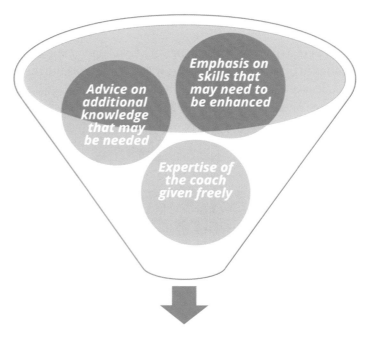

Development towards future success of the staff member

Figure 5.7 The fundamentals of a coaching approach

That is not to say, however, that coaching never has a part in the process of supervision. When a supervisor recognises talent and potential in a supervisee they may get involved in the process of coaching that supervisee to help them advance in their career trajectory in a manner that instigates direction, involvement and focus on the outcome for the supervisee. Coaching can include the facilitation of experiences that will be of benefit for the supervisee as they progress. For example, involving a supervisee in planning meetings on new procedures can help ensure that they will be ready and informed for the next step in the process of integrating the new procedures. Coaching has an element of personal involvement, in contrast to professional supervision, which is objective. Coaching would be more realistic as a follow-on from a supervision process where strengths and potential have already been developed, acknowledged and observed.

Structuring supervision

One of the most important aspects of any setting's approach to supervision is that robust, clearly understood and easy-to-follow structures are in place to support the process and that everybody involved is aware of their individual roles and responsibilities in making supervision work effectively. This does not happen without proper planning and an understanding of the need for a supervision process.

SUPERVISION POLICY

The Child Care Act 1991 (Early Years Services) Regulations 2016 mandates a written supervision policy in ELC settings.

* **Regulation 9** requires the registered ELC provider to ensure that staff are appropriately supervised in order to fulfil all the regulatory requirements of the setting itself.

* **Regulation 10** requires every setting to have a clear written policy and procedure on staff supervision.

Every setting has the legal responsibility to have a developed, structured written policy around the supervision practices and procedures in the setting. Failure to do so can result in the closure of the setting for breach of the Child Care Act 1991 (Early Years Services) Regulations 2016. Tusla's sample supervision policy, which can be adapted for settings' specific needs, can be seen in Appendix 1. As Tusla carries out inspections of ELC settings it makes practical sense that every person in an ELC setting is familiar with Tusla's draft policies, which are accessible at www.tusla.ie.

What is clear from the Tusla sample supervision policy are these specific requirements:

* An initial discussion process about the concept of supervision, what it entails and what can be expected from the process

* Clear written understanding between the supervisor and supervisee about exactly what the supervision process will and will not involve

* A schedule of time, place and scope for the supervision process

* Supervision sessions that are regular, consistent and uninterrupted

* An expectation that the supervision sessions will last for at least one hour (this may alter depending on the level of development of the supervisee, i.e. whether they are a beginner, intermediate or advanced supervisee)

* An agenda for each meeting which will be agreed in advance

* A record of the meeting will be made and signed by both the supervisor and the supervisee and it will be securely filed in accordance with the record-keeping policy and the confidentiality policy of the setting.

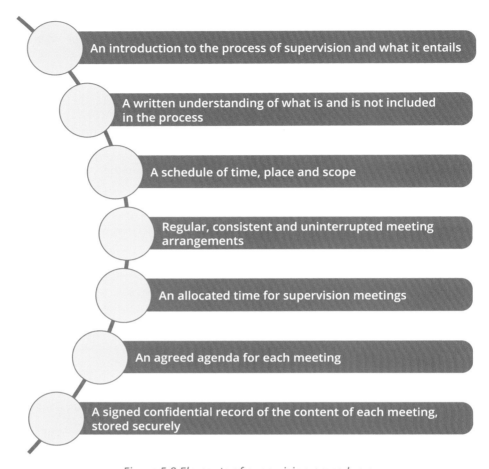

An introduction to the process of supervision and what it entails

A written understanding of what is and is not included in the process

A schedule of time, place and scope

Regular, consistent and uninterrupted meeting arrangements

An allocated time for supervision meetings

An agreed agenda for each meeting

A signed confidential record of the content of each meeting, stored securely

Figure 5.8 Elements of supervision procedures

INTRODUCING THE PROCESS OF SUPERVISION AND WHAT IT ENTAILS

There is a clear expectation that the supervisor and the supervisee will develop a specific type of working relationship, specifically one that is dialogic/discursive rather than didactic/ordering. This requires trust that is based on both knowing what they can expect to happen and, more importantly, accepting the process without fear or worry. The job of the supervisor at the start of this process is to clearly outline what is expected of the supervisee and the reasoning behind those expectations. Fundamental to this relationship of trust is the expectation that the supervisor has the expertise to carry out the process of supervision and has had training and experience around the needs of the task. This should be outlined to the supervisee so that they know the expertise that is being put in place to support their steps towards developing as professionals.

A number of competencies support the development of good supervisors. They should be:

* An active listener

* Confident but aware of their own limitations and skillsets

* Well informed about the ELC sector and the setting's standards

* Prepared to be accountable, approachable and enabling

* Able to spot talent and learning needs for others

* A strategic thinker and problem solver

* Supportive and collegial

* Collaborative

* A team builder, goal setter and future planner.

One particularly important part of professional supervision is the one-to-one support that enables the supervisee review their own practice in an enabling, constructive, non-judgemental way. It supports wellbeing and the setting's values and mission and ensures that the supervisee has an opportunity to constructively explore issues they might wish to bring to the discussion as part of their own journey.

As outlined in Chapter 4, it should also be explained to supervisees that they may require different intensities of supervision, depending on their level of development (Stoltenberg & Delworth 1987). It should also be understood that situations may arise in the actual setting or the ELC sector where supervision may need to be reactivated and the intensity increased and that this is not necessarily a reflection on the supervisee but is a result of changing circumstances. This is a process that reflects what Argyris and Schön (1996) describe as double-loop learning within experiential learning.

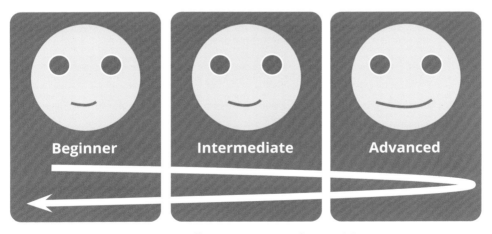

Figure 5.9 Different intensities of supervision

It is important that at every stage each supervisee feels comfortable with the process they are involved in as part of supervision, which helps to ensure that the best possible use of the time and learning can be made. The supervisor should at the outset explain the systems, structures and procedures as well as ensuring that the limitations are clearly understood by everybody. In this case preparation produces progress for all.

THINK AND REFLECT

Reflect on your last month in placement/practicum and explain, based on your experiences, what you would do to prepare for a supervision session in your work placement/practicum.

* What items would you like to put on the agenda?

* What items would you leave out and why would you leave them out?

A MEMORANDUM OF UNDERSTANDING

When discussing the process of supervision, many people refer to the need for a contract of supervision, but it is important to be aware of the legal implications of the concept of a 'contract' (offer, acceptance, legality, etc.) and it is therefore preferable to discuss a 'memorandum' or 'agreement', which just as succinctly outlines the processes involved. For this reason I will use the term 'memorandum of understanding'.

Every supervision system should, in a written memorandum of understanding, outline the basics of what should be expected of both the supervisor and the supervisee as joint contributors to supervision. The memorandum itself will often determine the effectiveness of the procedures that are put in place for supervision in a setting and contribute to the success for everyone involved.

A sample template of a supervision memorandum of understanding can be seen in Appendix 2. While it illustrates the items to be included, it should not be relied upon without consultation, planning and engagement with the supervisee.

A memorandum of understanding should include the following:

* The names and positions and record of acceptance of each participant – the supervisor and supervisee.

* The purpose of supervision in relation to the supervisee, supervisor and the individual setting.

* An outline of preparation required by both supervisor and supervisee for each session in order to ensure that time is used effectively.

* A list of the limitations of what will, could and should be discussed in supervision.

* The overall approach to be taken in the supervision.

* The frequency of supervision.
* An outline of where the supervision will take place and the expected duration of each session.
* An understanding of who will prepare the agenda and when that agenda will be agreed prior to each session.
* Acceptance of the recording of the session in the agreed style (not verbatim), bearing in mind that it is a 'snapshot' taken at a particular time in the supervisee's process of reflection and review.
* An undertaking that what happens in the session of supervision is confidential to the participants.
* Outline of the security arrangements in relation to the notes of the sessions.
* A timeline for the review of the memorandum of agreement to ensure that it is fit for the purpose it is designed for and for the development needs of the supervisee.
* An outline of what circumstances would lead to the cancellation of the supervision process.

Different memoranda may be required for different modes of supervision, but the overall concept of an agreed structure will determine the content of each mode of supervision used in the setting. The above list is indicative rather than prescriptive.

THINK AND REFLECT

Look at the elements in the template of a memorandum of agreement for supervision and explain the significance of each section.

What do you think might be added to make the agreement more relevant to your setting's needs?

Are there any sections you would reword? Why?

A SCHEDULE OF TIME, PLACE AND SCOPE

Supervision sessions should take place somewhere private, comfortable and free from distractions. It should encourage a relaxed atmosphere, which will contribute to the interchange of reflection, discussion and action planning that will take place in the session. It should be clear that when the session is in progress the participants are not to be disturbed. Those involved in the session should be fully available, committed, open to the reflective discussions that are taking place and free to engage at their own pace without interruption. It is important to hold sessions regularly so that meaningful reflection is possible and the issues arising are fresh and easy to recall when being reviewed, discussed and actioned.

In relation to scope, the issues discussed in each supervision session should be relevant and developmental for the supervisee; therefore there should be some inbuilt focus to the discussions which should be agreed in advance by both supervisor and supervisee. Personal gripes, holiday plans and suchlike should not be brought into work supervision sessions.

A template for recording place, time and attendance at supervision can be seen in Appendix 3. Such a record should be retained in each individual's supervision file so that it is easy to note the time, place and duration of each supervision session. This should be initialled by each participant. If the time and/or place needs to be changed, this should also be noted in case patterns emerge that could be a topic for discussion in the supervision sessions when they do take place.

REGULAR, CONSISTENT AND UNINTERRUPTED MEETING ARRANGEMENTS

Just recording when supervision takes place is not the same as committing to the regulatory requirements for the process to be ongoing and consistent. The difference between this aspect and the preceding one of place, time and scope is the element of

pre-planning of the sessions to ensure that interruptions do not impinge on the effectiveness of ongoing and dialogic discussions that should be envisaged as part of supervision. This requires both the supervisor and the supervisee to actually clear the time for the meeting that is envisaged and to be clear in their minds that the supervision will take place and ensure that they are open to the discussions that are to take place. It also requires there to be an agenda of what is proposed to be part of the supervision discussions. Any agenda should be agreed mutually and should allow for either the supervisee or supervisor to add an item to the discussion list. This makes for a fully participatory process that is more likely to be productive and formative for the supervisee in particular.

AN ALLOCATED TIME FOR SUPERVISION MEETINGS

The length of time needed for each supervision meeting should be clear to all involved and should form part of the supervision agreement. Time should be 'banked' at regular intervals for the supervision meetings to take place. The amount of time needed for each supervisee will depend on the needs of that supervisee and should be negotiated through the supervision agreement or supervision memorandum.

The need for specific time allocation will depend on the level of development of each supervisee (beginner, intermediate or advanced) to ensure that the appropriate amount of time can be allocated within the internal time management systems of the setting. While this may appear to be easy to predict, based on the experience of the supervisor (and theoretically it may well be), there should always be a contingency time built into the planning in case issues arise that change the level at which the supervisee finds themselves at the time of the supervision.

The time slots needed for each supervisee will be understood by experienced supervisors who know the working of their own settings, but a guide might be as follows.

Weekly sessions for	Newly starting staff
	Those requiring additional support
Bi-weekly sessions for	New staff who have some experience in other settings
	Newly promoted staff at a new grade
	Staff who are dealing with specific work challenges
Monthly sessions for	Experienced employees
	Employees who have advanced in their roles
	Employees who do not appear to need as much supervision and the supervisee

It is possible for an employee in each of these categories to advance or to revert to another time frequency for supervision as the need arises. A good supervisor who supports the needs of the supervisee will identify which category each supervisee fits into at any particular point in their professional development journey. It is important that the supervision time suits both the supervisor and the supervisee.

A MUTUALLY AGREED AGENDA FOR EACH MEETING

In order to ensure the efficient use of time and the effective content of supervision sessions, they should have planned agendas that are agreed in advance of the sessions. Fundamental to Morrison's 4x4x4 model of supervision is the embedded process of reflection, which requires the personal reflections of the supervisee on their experiences in the setting to inform the supervision session by allowing the issues that arise from those settings to feed into the agenda for the supervision session. This means that participants should know in advance what can be expected in the session and this can be based on the observations of either the supervisee or the supervisor outside of the supervision session.

The agenda can be a 'living document' – issues for the agenda can change as long as there is mutual agreement. Such changes should be notified in advance so that items that were planned can be reallocated to another discussion if the need arises. An effective way to prepare this is to keep a record of the previous meeting with agreed actions and who is nominated to undertake tasks agreed. This then forms the basis of the next meeting; but the need for advance notice, realistic tasks and scaffolding of learning embodied within the process should always be respected.

There are several approaches to the content and direction of each actual supervision session, which are informed by the need to develop the understanding, the level of knowledge and even the maturity of the supervisee in the process.

Methodology

The method used in individual sessions may depend on how comfortable the supervisor is with each process. A combination of methods or processes may be best for different situations, discussions, levels of engagement or confidence levels of the supervisee. There should not be a 'one size fits all' approach. For this reason, it is useful to look at some of the techniques that can be used in supervision.

SOCRATIC QUESTIONING

Socratic questioning forms the foundation of cognitive behavioural therapy (CBT), which uses a series of focused, open-ended questions to encourage a process of reflection (Clarke & Egan 2015). This helps the person to identify the impact of their beliefs and thoughts, and to examine the meaning of what they experience (Beck & Dozois 2011).

The process is focused on open-ended questions; yes/no replies are not options for answering the questions posed. Importantly, after the open-ended question is asked, the supervisee is allowed time to focus on how they will answer. This encourages them to reflect before they answer, allowing them to explore deeper thinking in the process. Then their answer is probed further, drawing the supervisee into deeper reasoning and understanding, and enabling existing assumptions to be examined, understood or modified in a natural way.

The process involves several steps:

* Clarifying meaning – e.g. *What exactly does that mean?*
* Clarifying assumptions – e.g. *How can you verify that assumption?*
* Digging deeper – e.g. *How do you know that?*
* Exploring implications – e.g. *How does that fit with what you have already learned?*
* Developing positions or viewpoints – e.g. *Can this be looked at another way?*

The process of deeper questioning should be explained before it starts so that new supervisees in particular, who may not be confident, understand why the process is being adopted so that it does not seem like an interrogation, which would be intimidating. Additionally, as the supervisee is exploring deeper thoughts, they need to feel safe in the process. They should know that the thoughts they express are natural and logical stages in their professional development.

Extend Your Learning

 Read more about Socratic questioning so that you understand the process. See www.intel.com/content/dam/www/program/education/us/en/documents/project-design/strategies/dep-question-socratic.pdf.

THINK AND REFLECT

Divide into working groups and draw up a list of questions that you think would work in a supervision session to bring a new supervisee into deeper conversation.

PROFESSIONAL CAPABILITIES FRAMEWORK

This is an established method of exploring capabilities in social work and can be adapted for those working in the ELC sector. It is built around nine specific domains:

Figure 5.10 The nine domains of the professional capabilities framework

Each topic in the nine domains suggests its own questions for discussion. For example, a topic for enquiry under rights, justice and economic wellbeing could be:

* Are there any issues around protecting the rights of the child in the situation we are discussing?

* What support do you think this child might need to exercise their equality rights in the situation we are discussing?

Focusing on each of the nine domains prompts an in-depth analysis of issues that arise and discourages superficial answers. In application the nine domains are represented by flashcards, one for each discussion or questioning prompt. A card can be selected randomly so that there is variety and non-predictability about the discussions that happen in the supervision session. Thus, a card is picked at random and that directs where the discussion goes. Then another card could be selected to broaden the discussion.

THINK AND REFLECT

1   Create nine domain cards (see the list above) and design a list of questions for the back of each card which will draw out discussion of the domain selected.

2   Design a PowerPoint presentation to explain your choices and how you decided on the questions that you came up with for each card.

MACLEAN'S HEAD, HEART, HANDS AND FEET

Cameron (2005) describes the concept of 'head, heart and hands' as a supervision technique which supports supervisees to reflect on the skills and knowledge they bring to situations. 'Head' is where the knowledge is processed and it represents the bank of theories on which practice is based; 'heart' is about the sense of belonging a supervisee would feel in their setting; and 'hands' relates to the skills the supervisee has and how they choose to use them.

Ingram (2013) added the concept of 'feet', which relates to ethical and professional learning, ensuring that the supervisee works ethically and develops a professional sense of belonging.

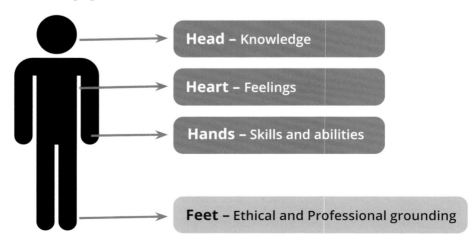

Figure 5.11 Head, heart, hands and feet (adapted from Cameron 2005 and Ingram 2013)

Maclean proposed using prompt cards for social workers based on the head, heart, hands and feet to prompt discussions around the four concepts and these can be useful in introducing supervisees to the thought processes that will underpin their developing practice (Maclean 2015). Once again, there is no single 'correct' methodology but there are a variety of methods to stimulate the transfer, discussion and personal journey of each supervisee depending on what best suits their developing levels of reflection on their work, their influence and their sense of ownership of their own professionalism.

Extend Your Learning

 Research the following methodologies and list three advantages and three challenges they pose in their use as methodologies for reflection in supervision:

* Munro's Decision Tree

* De Bono's Thinking Hats

The list of analysis tools that can be used in supervision grows as expertise and research on the process of supervision grows, and we can expect that new tools will continue to be embraced by settings to suit their supervisees, whatever their individual needs. Whatever methodology is employed in the ELC setting should be selected carefully based on the needs of the setting and the supervisee and the skills of the supervisor, and therefore careful thought should be given to which methodology or methodologies are used.

Recording and planning

Returning to the agenda of a supervision meeting and the record of the meeting, having examined some of the methodologies that can be used in individual supervision sessions, it is easy to understand why issues could arise that might need to be revisited later. There may be a need to reflect more deeply in another session, or a newer or alternative methodology may be better suited to a later supervision session. For this reason records of supervision do need to be retained to facilitate further development or discussion. They should be agreed and signed off by both supervisor and supervisee and any anomalies or dissatisfaction recorded appropriately.

The record should include what was planned to be discussed (the **agenda**), what was actually discussed (the **record**) and what is intended to be discussed going forward (the **plan**). Using the ARP (agenda, record, plan) approach creates a 'living document' that develops through each supervision session for each supervisee as they develop their knowledge, professional stance and sense of belonging to the setting in which the supervision takes place. A simple working record using ARP can be seen in Appendix 4.

CONFIDENTIALITY

It is important to the integrity of the process of supervision, and the trust developed in the supervision process by the supervisee in particular, that the records of supervision sessions are confidential. This is particularly important as they are records of the personal development journey of each supervisee. They must be stored in a secure place and procedures must be in place to ensure that only those who need to access the records can do so.

However, ensuring that the records are kept securely is not a guarantee that others cannot access those files and this should be explained to the supervisee. Access should only be allowed to those who can show that they have a legitimate interest in the content, for example the supervisor's line manager, Tusla, or some other investigative agency where a need arises to make the detail accessible. Thus the concept of confidentiality is not an absolute, and this should form part of the discussions between supervisor and supervisee at the time that the Supervision Memorandum or Supervision Agreement is being negotiated.

Notwithstanding necessary access as outlined above it is fundamental to the integrity of supervision that records are promptly completed, signed off on by both the supervisor and the supervisee and then stored securely to protect their confidentiality.

As with all personal records in organisations and under the requirements of the General Data Protection Regulation 2018 (GDPR), there should also be a record retention policy in every organisation. Where personal data is stored it is imperative that if a person were to leave the specific ELC setting, their record can only be retained for as long as the setting's record retention policy states and not beyond that (unless in circumstances exempted by law and the GDPR). After the retention policy's stated period the record should be destroyed.

Finally, in the records of supervision it should not be possible to name individuals who are not part of the supervision exchange. Where other names arise in the discussions that take place in the supervision session, they should be anonymised (i.e. initials only should be used in the record).

CASE STUDY

Jennifer is a supervisor in an ELC setting. She has a QQI Level 8 qualification in ECEC and is a very high achiever, as evidenced by her setting numbers, which have been increasing every year for the last three years. There is a waiting list for the setting and many parents are disappointed when they are unable to get a place for their children. Jennifer is a highly conscientious worker and has put a lot of work into a supervision process for all her staff.

It is August and several of Jennifer's staff have handed in their notice over the last two weeks. She does not know why they are leaving and wonders if there is something wrong with her supervision processes; these resignations have come out of the blue. She is also worried because new children will be starting in September and she must recruit staff quickly.

Can you advise Jennifer on what she should do and whether there are any changes she should incorporate in the setting?

CASE STUDY

Fidelity has for the last two years been a supervisor in a small setting that is run by two staff members.

Fidelity's boss has just informed her that she has bought the premises beside them and has secured planning permission to triple the size of the setting. The boss has asked Fidelity to draw up a plan for six new staff members and to design a job advertisement for the new staff members.

What should Fidelity consider in her plans for the new premises and staff, particularly in relation to the supervision of the new recruits?

How should Fidelity go about the process and what documents does she need?

Recap

1. **List five benefits of a placement/practicum.**

2. **What is Socratic questioning and what are its strengths?**

3. **What are the nine domains of the professional capabilities framework?**

4. **Explain the effect on supervision of the level of development of supervisees.**

5. **List five different models of supervision in ELC and give a brief description of each.**

References and further reading

Argyris, C. and Schön, D. (1996) *Organisational Learning: Theory, Method and Practice*. Reading MA: Addison-Wesley

Beck, A. and Dozois, D. (2011) Cognitive therapy: 'Current status and future directions' *Annual Review of Medicine* 62: 397-407

Brookfield, S. (1995) *Becoming a Critically Reflective Teacher*. California: Jossey-Bass

Brown, L. and Turney, D. (2014). *Analysis and Critical Thinking in Assessment* (2nd edn.) Dartington: Research in Practice

Cameron, C. (2005) 'With heart, head and hands', *Community Care*, 16 August

Clarke, G. and Egan, S. (2015) 'The Socratic method in cognitive behavioural therapy: A narrative review', *Cognitive Therapy and Research* 39(6): 863–79

Gibbs, G. (1988) *Learning by Doing: A Guide to Teaching and Learning Methods*. Oxford: Further Education Unit, Oxford Polytechnic

Huggins, S. (2017) 'Practice-based learning in LIS education: An overview of current trends', *Library Trends* 66(1): 13–22

Ingram, R. (2013) 'Emotions, social work practice and supervision: An uneasy alliance?' *Journal of Social Work Practice* 27(1): 5-19

King, A. (1993) 'Sage on the stage to guide on the side', *College Teaching* 41(1), (Winter): 30–5

Lave, J. and Wenger, E. (1991). *Situated Learning: Legitimate Peripheral Participation*. Cambridge: Cambridge University Press

Maclean, S. (2015) *Reflective Practice Cards: Prompt Cards for Social Workers*. Lichfield: Kirwen Maclean Associates.

Morrison, T. (2005) *Staff Supervision in Social Care*. Brighton: Pavilion

Munro, E., Cartwright, N., Hardie, J. and Matuschi, E. (2016) *Improving Child Safety: Deliberation, Judgement and Empirical Research*. Durham: Centre for Humanities Engaging Science and Society (CHESS)

Stoltenberg, C. and Delworth, U. (1987) *Supervising Counsellors and Therapists: A Developmental Approach*. San Francisco CA: Jossey-Bass

Taylor, C. and White, S. (2006) 'Knowledge and reasoning in social work: Educating for humane judgement', *British Journal of Social Work* 36: 937–54

Wenger, E. (1998) *Communities of Practice: Learning, Meaning and Identity*. Cambridge: Cambridge University Press

Whitmore, J. (2009) *Coaching for Performance*. London: Nicholas Brearley

6

Supervision and its Implications in ELC Settings

Introduction

By now you will understand that embedding supervision in any ELC setting, and understanding the process and procedures, ensures that the experience is a positive one for all stakeholders. Therefore it is important that both supervisors and supervisees take the time necessary to embed a clear understanding of the part each plays in the success of the process. This can be done as set out in Chapter 5.

Additionally, you should now understand how supervision contributes to the evolving professional sense of belonging for new supervisees, who are supported in their development within not just the setting, but the profession of ELC practitioners.

There are, however, other considerations to be taken into account when examining the importance of good supervision practices in ELC settings.

Duty of care

Section 8 of the Safety, Health and Welfare at Work Act 2005 places a legal obligation on employers to take whatever measures are practicable to protect the safety, health and welfare of all their employees. This is a wide-ranging responsibility and the Act requires that employers risk assess the activities their employees are involved in, put procedures in place to reduce any potential harm that could arise, and ensure that the employee is at the centre of harm prevention measures (including training and support) that should be put in place where practicable to reduce the possibility of harm being done to the employee.

Where staff in an ELC setting are unsupported in their work there is a danger that they might become overwhelmed by issues that could arise, particularly in relation to the inherent vulnerability of the children they work with, which can cause stress or adverse psychological responses. For this reason it is a legal responsibility for every operator of an ELC setting to ensure that training and support are provided to prevent that potential risk. It is part of their duty of care to their staff and indeed to the children in their charge and their parents/guardians. Supervision is a fundamental, and legally required, part of that duty of care under the Safety, Health and Welfare at Work Act 2005. Failure by any employer to comply with the requirements of the Act may lead to potential financial and/or criminal sanctions for that employer.

Regulations

CHILD CARE ACT 1991 (EARLY YEARS SERVICES) REGULATIONS 2016

Regulation 9 of the Child Care Act 1991 (Early Years Services) Regulations 2016 states that registered providers of early years services (which includes ELC settings) must ensure that staff are appropriately supervised in relation to all the regulatory requirements for the service. Thus supervision is recognised as a basic requirement for all registered service providers. Under Regulation 10, a supervision policy must be in a clear written format (see Appendix 1 for an example). Not every written policy has to be exactly the same, but the template produced by Tusla (www.tusla.ie; search under Sample Policies and Templates) lists the fundamental items a supervision policy should include to outline the procedures and their application within a specific setting.

TUSLA

Tusla's *Quality and Regulatory Framework* (2018) outlines the need for a robust supervision policy in all settings. As part of the registration requirements for every

ELC setting in Ireland, Tusla's inspectorate will check that one is in place in every setting they visit and that it is regularly reviewed. The supervision policy in any ELC setting should be a 'live working document'; i.e. it should be updated and reviewed regularly and changes made where needed, to ensure that it is suitable for both staff and children and that it encourages the developing process of embedding professionalism and professionalisation developments in ELC in Ireland.

Morrison's 4x4x4 positive outcomes

As we have seen, Morrison's 4x4x4 model of supervision (Morrison 2005) has been recognised as the most relevant model for ELC settings. It has at its core the reflection that ELC staff are familiar with as part of their professional practice.

Strongly embedding the 4x4x4 model has positive effects in every setting, as outlined by Morrison (2005) and is described as the Seven Links (Barnardos 2020, p. 8).

THE SEVEN LINKS

1. *Role clarity* – people are clear about what is required of them in the task they undertake.
2. *Role security* – people feel that their job is sustainable and the setting has confidence in their ability to do the job.
3. *Empathy* – the worker feels they understand what is required and they feel they are part of a team and can contribute to the success of that team.
4. *Observation and Assessment* – people grow more aware of what they should do and display confidence to the extent that they can make a contribution independently.
5. *Partnership* – workers align themselves with the goals, ideas and plans of the organisation.
6. *Planning* – the worker feels that their contribution is valued and they take ownership of the processes in the setting.
7. *Coaching/Intervention* – the worker feels that they can give advice and as a result begin to grow within the supervision process from a foundational perspective.

(Adapted from Barnardos 2020)

Examining the outcomes outlined by Morrison and Barnardos, depicted more visually in Figure 6.1, it is easy to see that the positive outcomes are based on the development of confident, contributing and capable staff members who can enhance the professional work of every other staff member in an ELC setting.

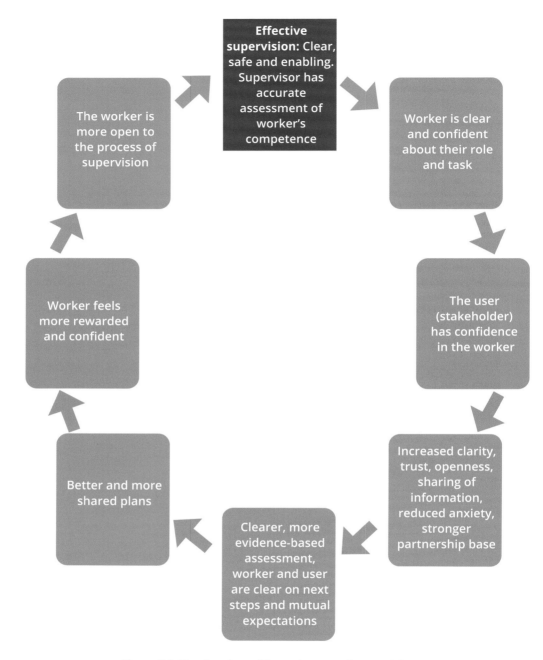

Figure 6.1 Morrison's positive outcomes of supervision

The contribution of supervision to organisational culture in the ELC setting

Culture in an organisation relates to 'an organisation's values, beliefs, practices, rituals and customs' (Marguardt 2002). It is therefore the thing that creates a sense of identity for those who work in the organisation. It includes the rituals and ways of doing things that are often only seen and experienced by the people in the organisation. In the words of Schein, 'perhaps the most intriguing aspect of culture as a concept is that it points you to phenomena that are below the surface, that are powerful in their impact but invisible and to a considerable degree unconscious' (Schein, 2004 p. 8).

For Schein there are competing aspects of culture:

* **Artefacts** – The range of procedures and behaviours that are seen as normal and acceptable and that are easy to spot as they are visibly manifested in the way people in organisations are seen to behave.

* **Shared beliefs and values** – These are less visible but when they exist they point to a sense of collectiveness that is shared by everyone in the organisation.

* **Fundamental assumptions or beliefs** – These are less visible as they are deeply held and personal to the people in the organisation.

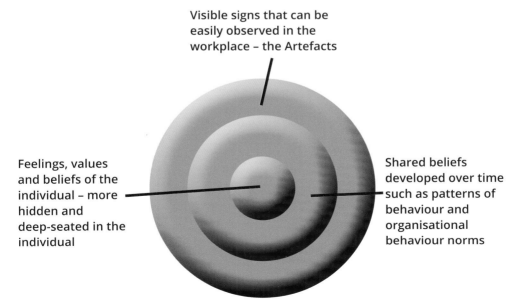

Visible signs that can be easily observed in the workplace – the Artefacts

Feelings, values and beliefs of the individual – more hidden and deep-seated in the individual

Shared beliefs developed over time such as patterns of behaviour and organisational behaviour norms

Figure 6.2 Competing aspects of culture (adapted from Schein 2004)

It is the competing nature of these elements that builds our understanding of how cultures develop in organisations and how the aspects of experience within the organisation can affect the overall 'feel' of the organisation for others who observe its practices and procedures. In the case of ELC settings these feelings can be palpable and affect how children, their parents/guardians and other stakeholders feel about a setting.

The culture of a setting can be collaborative and positive or challenged and compromised. We might be tempted to use the expressions 'positive culture' or 'negative culture' but this would be misleading. Whatever the culture, the work still gets done; it's just that what we might call 'the vibe' may lead one to suspect that all is not working well beneath the surface. It may take a long time for the real issues to be articulated and they may never be articulated – people might just leave the setting without addressing the issues.

COLLABORATIVE POSITIVE CULTURE

A collaborative positive culture invites participation, commitment, learning and trust-building. Problems or challenges are faced with shared processes that assist the organisation to develop a 'can-do' attitude. For children in a collaboratively focused culture there is consistency, openness and supportive structures, and staff act as positive role models. Strengths are celebrated and where weaknesses or challenges arise they are openly acknowledged. All staff at all levels in the setting work collectively towards positive outcomes.

A collaborative approach results in:

* Clear and open values and goals

* Positive leadership processes

* Clear policies, procedures and standards that everyone understands

* Effective training and engagement

* Positive internal and external channels of communication.

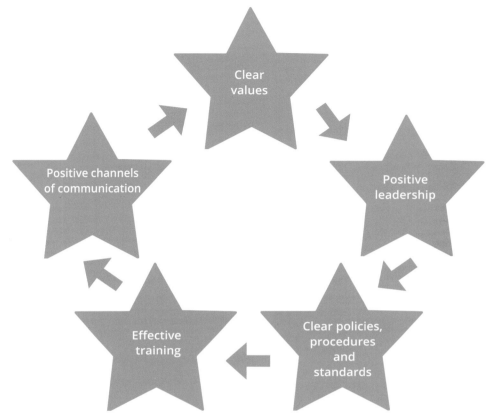

Figure 6.3 Indicators of collaborative positive culture

COMPROMISED AND CHALLENGED CULTURES

In these cultures there is often an overemphasis on getting on with the job; following the rules; working on despite being stressed or anxious; and covering over any cracks – 'nothing to see here, folks'. In such a culture, staff can develop a defensive attitude, which can become institutionalised (Menzies 1970).

Change is not trusted and self-defence ensures that things are done as they have always been done without innovation – nobody 'rocks the boat'. It is a type of organisational culture that stifles progress, trust and confidence-building. For staff in such organisations:

* There can be a 'them and us' approach.

* Stakeholders are not encouraged or interested in engaging.

* There is a defensive approach because of the fear of blame being apportioned to staff members.

* Stress and anxiety may be overwhelming and can often result in high staff turnover and low morale.

* Dependence on management can be prevalent as staff are afraid to take actions or make independent decisions, no matter how much experience they have.

* There may be a reluctance to be open and truthful where consequences are feared.

* Where problems arise a 'quick fix' approach may be adopted to avoid exposure of the real roots of the problem.

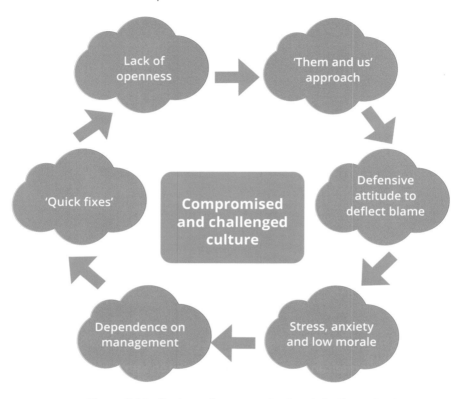

Figure 6.4 Indicators of compromised and challenged cultures

Examples of compromised and challenged cultures and how they arise include:

Figure 6.5 Approaches that help create compromised and challenged cultures
(adapted from Davys & Beddoe 2010)

EFFECTS OF SUPERVISION APPROACHES ON CULTURE IN ELC SETTINGS

Davys and Beddoe examined categories of effect on culture that arise when organisations are challenged and compromised (Davys & Beddoe 2010). Issues arise because the management or owners overlook the importance of ensuring that the whole organisation is included and invested in developing, and understanding at a deep level, the fundamental beliefs, feelings and values that are at the heart of positive culture-building in the organisation. In ELC settings this concept is fundamental to the mission and value statement that parents/guardians examine when they consider an ELC setting's suitability for their children.

Embedding these fundamental beliefs, feelings and values is one of the most important parts of great supervision and those who experience such supervision will become invested in their own development and the strength of purpose of the setting in which they operate.

What is evident in compromised/challenged cultures in relation to supervision is that there is a mismatch between the development of organisational processes and the messages that result or are misinterpreted and this creates a void, preventing effective implementation of good, enabling supervision in the organisation.

Essentially, 'members of the organisation adopt forms of behaviour that they feel are appropriate to them under the circumstances imposed on them by the organisational holding environment' (Stapley 1996, p. 40). The void is as much about what is said as it is about what is unsaid, but it exposes anomalies between intention and practice and needs to be regularly revisited and questioned so that change, if needed, can be effected.

CASE STUDY

Amelia is a supervisor at Cheeky ELC and has held that position for five years. The setting has six rooms and has a very good reputation with people in the locality. Children are happy and there is a focus on play, inclusion and preparing children for transition to the nearby school with the aim of giving every child the best chance to succeed in their education at that school.

For the last few weeks Amelia has been concerned about how one child has been settling in. The child's parents have expressed some concern that the child does not want to go to the setting every morning and Amelia has also noticed that the child seems to be very quiet whenever she visits the room.

This morning, when Amelia went into the room the child in question was sitting alone with his back to the wall and seemed watchful. The two staff in the room were ignoring him and appeared to be arguing. When Amelia asked why the child was not involved with the activities the other children were doing, the staff members both said that they were fed up working in that room and couldn't agree on anything. They felt it would be better if they were moved. The child was a problem as he wouldn't take part in activities so they just left him until he was more used to what was done. He didn't speak to the other children either.

Amelia was shocked by their answer but she knows that she has to do something. What do you think Amelia will do? How do you think she will go about it?

To enable change, it is important to elicit feedback regularly from those in the supervision delivery and practice process and not to gloss over any issues that might arise in that feedback. Thinking around the issues also encourages ownership and engagement by everyone involved.

Good supervision procedures and experiences for staff contribute to many positives in a setting and encourage a respect for learning, development and a habit of questioning procedures that do not work or challenges that need to be addressed by all staff in a setting. The benefits for staff are a well-developed sense of belonging, feeling valued and supported; being committed to learning; and being professional and supportive to all within the setting.

CASE STUDY

Matilda has arrived for her scheduled supervision session with a list of twenty things she wants to 'bring to the table' regarding her work in the baby room. One item is that she has been asked to stay late every day for the last month because a parent has needed to work late to get a new project finished, meaning that she is picking up her child late every day. She seems to have agreed with 'somebody' that this is okay. Matilda has only been working for the setting for the last eight months and feels that she is being taken advantage of.

How do you think Matilda's supervisor, Emma, should respond to the long list of items? How, do you think, should matters progress?

Recap

1. **Name the Seven Links outlined by Barnardos (2020).**

2. **List five advantages of a collaborative positive culture.**

3. **Contrast a collaborative positive culture with a compromised and challenged culture.**

4. **Write a blog for the setting on how you and all the stakeholders in the setting support the culture of the setting (max. 150 words).**

References and further reading

Barnardos (2020) *Supervision and Support in Early Learning and Care*. Dublin: Barnardos

Davys, A. and Beddoes, L. (2010) *Best Practice in Professional Supervision: A Guide for the Helping Professions*. London: Jessica Kingsley

Gibbs, G. (1988) *Learning by Doing: A Guide to Teaching and Learning Methods*. Oxford: Further Education Unit, Oxford Polytechnic

Marguardt, M. (2002) *Building the Learning Organisation*. New York: McGraw-Hill

Menzies, I. (1970) *The Functioning of Social Systems as a Defence against Anxiety*. London: Tavistock Institute of Human Relations

Morrison, T. (2005) *Staff Supervision in Social Care*. Brighton: Pavilion

Schein, E. (2004) *Organizational Culture and Leadership* (3rd edn). San Francisco CA: Jossey-Bass

Stapley, L. (1996) *The Personality of the Organisation*. London: Free Association Books

Tusla (2018) *Quality and Regulatory Framework*. Dublin: Early Years Inspectorate, Tusla

Section 3

The Setting

7

The Qualities of a Supervisor

Learning Goals

In this chapter, learners will:

* Examine some of the qualities of good supervisors in ELC

* Examine the complexities of the job of a supervisor and the complexities of children's lives

* Look at the planning involved in CPD requirements in an ELC setting

Introduction

One of the fundamental aspects of any supervisor's job in ELC is to create the environmental culture (as we have seen) and to support the delicate balance between the needs of the ELC, the fundamental rights and needs of the children in the setting, the best interests of those children and their parents/guardians and the administrative processes involved in the day-to-day organisation of the work that is carried out in the setting.

As we saw in Chapter 6, the careful balancing of all aspects of supervision can have huge impacts on all stakeholders in the setting. Figure 7.1 gives some insight into the different aspects of a supervisor's job. In the diagram the cogs do not go round neatly and smoothly but by misaligned elements that sometimes turn other than you might expect. This is due to the nature of the aspects involved – sometimes things go neatly and rhythmically, but there is no guarantee, even if you do everything correctly, that there will be no stumbling blocks. The supervisor may have to reinvent a whole process because of one spanner in the works, but a skilled, informed and savvy supervisor will show their true abilities when things are not perfect.

In this section we look at the role of the supervisor and how their work contributes to the overall operation of the setting.

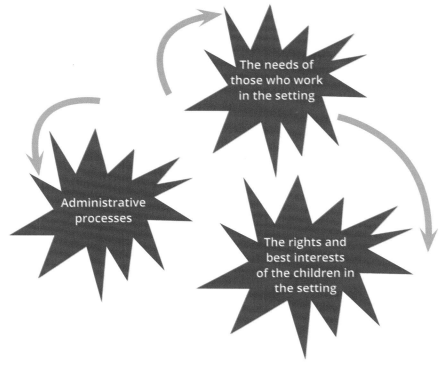

Figure 7.1 Aspects of a supervisor's job in ELC

Qualities, skills and competencies of an ELC supervisor

To be effective in an ELC setting, it is imperative that the supervisor is aware of all aspects of the job they do and how their own qualities, skills and competencies can be applied to their work.

Not only does the supervisor have to manage the complex requirements of the supervision process for all levels of supervisee, as we have outlined in earlier chapters; they also have to manage their own position in relation to the numerous stakeholders in the setting while also:

✱ Ensuring that the care and learning of each child in the setting is of the highest standard

✱ Keeping up to date with developments in one of the most rapidly developing sectors in Ireland

✱ Ensuring that the welfare and wellbeing of children and colleagues is paramount

✱ Supervising CPD, staff development and personal enrichment and motivation for all staff members

* Empowering staff to give of their best on a daily basis

* Timetabling, budgeting, advertising, reception, supporting, advocating, mediating, directing; and embedding equality, equity, diversity, fun, learning, play, literacy, numeracy, development and empowerment for all

* Engaging and partnering with parents in the setting, in the interests of their children

* Meeting regulatory and legislative requirements

* Managing funding application requirements

* Envisioning future needs in relation to staffing, teaching and learning and succession.

Figure 7.2 Complexity of the supervisor's role

This complexity, however, is manageable, as you will see in your practicum placements where you will meet and work with effective supervisors who meet these challenges through good planning, focus, learning and the ability to develop the skills needed for the tasks required.

All of the above complexities (and this list is not exhaustive) are further added to by the uniqueness of the children and their needs, which are paramount in the job that any supervisor does.

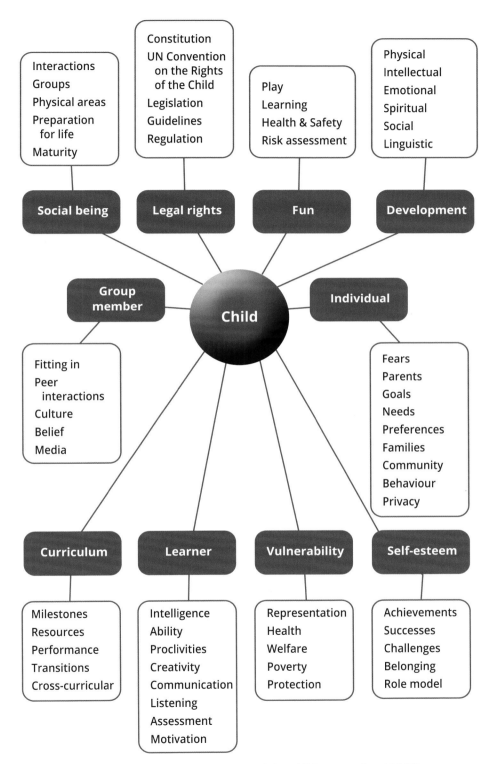

Figure 7.3 The complexity of the child (McPartland 2012)

Balancing the complexities of the job with the parallel complexities of the child and ensuring that the balance is seamless is one of the biggest challenges that every supervisor encounters in their working lives. Every good supervisor will realise that the foundation of what they do is the child in the ELC setting and that the systems within that setting are centred on the complexities of that task, which Figure 7.3 explores. These are the issues that are the cornerstone of everything they do every day.

> ### THINK AND REFLECT
>
> What skills and competencies would you bring to the role of supervisor in your setting? How could you develop and enhance those skills and competencies?

THE CARE AND LEARNING OF EACH CHILD IN THE SETTING

Each child in a setting will be at a unique stage of development. The procedures to support their care and learning are constantly developing, but this aspect of the job requires the supervisor to keep themselves informed of developments, research, the needs of each child in the setting and their parents'/guardians' support needs. Keeping up to date on developments and on changes as they are happening may be best supported by engaging in communities of practice or networks of children's care and learning organisations such as Barnardos, the National Council for Curriculum and Assessment (NCCA), etc.

Even during the process of supervision with staff in the setting, the paramount consideration for every supervisor must be the impact of their own practices on the children. Whatever happens in supervision itself, the impact of supporting all levels of staff to reach their potential is reflected in the success of the setting in ensuring that the children who are cared for are happy, supported, learning and developing; and, more importantly, that they have good role models in the setting. That process is based on professionalism, support, empathy, openness, honesty and the determination of the supervisor to ensure that the processes they use are building blocks for a great staff team and in turn a great ELC environment.

KEEPING UP TO DATE

The constantly evolving learning necessary for each supervisor should be based on their own reflective processes in which they may identify channels through which they can access supportive development information that may enhance their capabilities. However, they may also need to engage with strategic change procedures themselves to achieve change in the sector. To achieve this, each supervisor should value their own contribution, be aware of anything that needs to be changed and be prepared to help bring about those changes through their own contribution to the efforts of others in the sector.

Partaking in research is another way of engaging with effecting change in the sector. Keeping abreast with ongoing research such as the National Longitudinal Study of Children in Ireland (Growing Up in Ireland) can offer insights into children's experiences that may not have been considered before. Updates on research can be accessed by registering to receive alerts from the Department of Children, Equality, Disability, Integration and Youth (DCEDIY), which funds, publishes and acts on such research. Changes to practice emerge from such research, so being up to date with developments helps one to understand the motivations for change and their potential impact on the work in the ELC setting. It also ensures that the supervisor's practice remains relevant and the procedures in the setting are valued and valuable.

THINK AND REFLECT

Investigate the following organisations and identify what research they have published that could help inform you as a supervisor about developments that could impact on your ELC setting. Write an annotated bibliography on the ones you identify.

* Barnardos
* Early Childhood Ireland
* OECD
* Tusla
* Department of Education (DoE)
* NCCA

Can you identify any other sources?

Research may also be needed to solve a particular problem for one specific child. That can help create better outcomes for that child and may have a knock-on advantage for other children or indeed the whole setting. The supervisor must network with necessary agencies and keep abreast of their research to ensure they have the best information about choices and possibilities for everyone in the setting. The ultimate outcome is child-based, child-focused and child-enabling and is fundamental to the core work of any setting in the ECL sector.

SUPPORTING WELFARE AND WELLBEING

A healthy, valued and supported staff feel that they are valued and they are appreciated – and not just superficially. It is important that all staff understand their role in the ELC setting and are only expected to work at a level at which they are competent. This should be part of the process of getting to know the supervisee in supervision sessions; a skilled supervisor who listens carefully will be able to tease out whether the supervisee should advance to more responsibility and is capable of handling the responsibility without adverse effects on their health and wellbeing. This is fundamental to the caring and nurturing that staff are also entitled to.

That is not to say that every staff member should not be challenged and motivated; but they should not be burdened with onerous responsibility until they are able for it and they feel comfortable and knowledgeable about the level at which they are expected to operate. These levels are not linear and at any time a staff member may feel overwhelmed for any number of reasons which may or may not have to do with the work in the setting. They may have outside pressures which impact at specific times and if these issues have arisen and have been discussed within supervision, a caring, observant and enabling supervisor can discreetly support the supervisee.

CASE STUDY

Amy is a manager in an ELC setting. She is in the process of reviewing the practices of all staff members and she wants to ensure that her review is comprehensive. She has created a list which she feels should cover all the things that might arise and is in the process of putting together an information newsletter for all staff so that there will be a uniform approach in the setting.

As part of the process Amy has spoken to all the room supervisors about what she is doing and they have agreed with her that it is a great idea. It will make their jobs easier because things will have to be done 'by the book' after this process.

Do you think Amy's plan is a good idea? Why/why not?

Are there any points you would like Amy to consider in relation to her new process?

Are there any other people you think should be consulted in this process?

Is there anything that might impact on Amy's idea? Do you think there should be a timescale for the review?

ORGANISING CPD AND STAFF ENRICHMENT

Organising activities that will enhance the skills that staff already have through CPD is an important part of the supportive work of a supervisor in ELC settings. This ensures that staff skills are continually improved in ways that support the children, their parents/guardians and other stakeholders as well as ensuring that quality service is at the forefront of the setting.

Ensuring that staff receive necessary upskilling and reskilling ensures that every team in the ELC setting is challenged, informed and feels part of a continually changing sector and they will understand that the setting they work in values their own career path. Keeping people at entry-level status is not conducive to a great retention policy and unless staff feel they are progressing they will feel undervalued and may move quickly to other employers who will value their career.

The process of CPD can be identified and planned for during supervision:

CPD decision processes as part of supervision

Process	Considerations	Possibilities
Assess the needs of the person and the setting	Enables the supervisor to understand the staff member's strengths and needs	Work together to build a plan of targeted CPD activities for the setting and the staff member
Identify what needs to be learned for that individual supervisee	Plan some learning activities that have worked before and assess them against the individual supervisee's learning styles – justification should be mutually agreed	Identify how the learning can best be planned, how often, with whom and the best learning style for the supervisee, e.g. e-learning, time-out learning, mentoring or formal learning
Do a skills analysis to identify any elements of the supervisee's learning that could be enhanced	Evaluate every aspect of what has been learned already and how it is being implemented to identify any gaps in relation to the way in which the setting applies that learning	Complete a skills audit when supervision is being established and involve the supervisee in the process to learn about their goals for themselves and the setting so that both are aligned as much as possible
Set up the learning and oversee the outcomes	Record the developmental impact of the learning and reflect on its effectiveness for the supervisee	Keep a record of CPD – this becomes part of the supervisee's record of attainment and satisfaction of ELC sectoral regulatory and legislative requirements
Evaluate the impact of the learning interventions	Update the records and reflect with the supervisee on how the learning has affected their concept of their own skills and competencies	Mutual discussions about the effectiveness of the learning, the changes that have been implemented and certification should be retained for inspection and regulation purposes

In an ELC setting, it is the job of the supervisor to ensure that the funding for staff advancement is efficiently used and the outcomes recorded in a regulatorily compliant manner. The setting and the supervisee should understand the value of constant learning and development in the best interests of the supervisee, the children they work with and the setting.

EMPOWERING STAFF

Empowerment refers to power sharing, the delegation of power or authority to subordinates in the organisation (Hollander & Offerman 1990). Individuals who feel empowered in their work take ownership of their own part in that work and understand the effect they have on outcomes for everybody.

We have already discussed the different levels of development of supervisees (see page 55), and well-trained supervisors will be able to assess when a supervisee has begun to advance through the stages – beginner, intermediate and advanced. The supervisor can then identify opportunities and allow the supervisee to take on new challenges and responsibilities as they take tentative steps through those stages. Experience and knowledgeable direction by an astute supervisor can empower staff to be armed with the capabilities and support to take on more power within their own context and to review their performance when challenges are presented. Feeling empowered allows staff to reach higher targets and enhances their ownership of their own development.

Empowerment also supports job enrichment, which contributes to a supervisee's sense of belonging in the setting and can reduce stress and anxiety in the process. Feeling part of a team can motivate staff to contribute their best in every situation that presents itself. This enhances the concept of 'making progress', which can boost motivation, positive emotions and progression towards their goals (Amabile & Kramer 2011).

THINK AND REFLECT

Think about an incident during your placement that made you feel empowered. Describe what it was about the approach of your supervisor that gave you that sense of empowerment.

Were there any incidents that made you feel disempowered? How do you think that feeling could have been changed with different interventions?

TIMETABLING, BUDGETING AND STRATEGIC CONCEPTS

In every ELC setting where staff are rostered to ensure that child:carer ratios are maintained at all times, the allocation of staff to each room is vital to ensure compliance with regulations. The supervisor should be aware at all times of who is available and when relief staff may be needed (in the case of absence, for instance). These decisions have an impact on the finances of the setting and that can impact on the efficient use of valuable resources. They also ensure that workloads are fairly dispersed and that staff are supported and can support others by ensuring a matching of skills and needs.

Budgeting allows choices to be made that are soundly investigated, substantiated and robustly implemented and ensures that resources that need to be provided can be sourced, costed and acquired as necessary. The supervisor must make the economic case for changes or developments to the setting owner/operator and this must be properly thought out and justified if needed. This can only be done by knowing what impact certain expenditures will have on the overall operation of the setting and the supervisor is the person who has their hands on all aspects of the inner workings of that specific setting. Thus budgeting *to* change and budgeting *for* change are important skills which a supervisor must oversee. The impact of funding on the workings of the setting has implications for all stakeholders, including the supervisees who are being developed and, most important, the children, whose care is the centrepiece of every ELC setting.

ENGAGING WITH CHILDREN AND PARENTS/ GUARDIANS

Every ELC setting exists to provide a service to children and their parents/guardians and the position of every person who works in the setting is *in loco parentis* (in the place of a parent). The supervisor's job is to ensure that every person who works in the setting has that concept at the very heart of everything they do. Under our Constitution the duty to protect the child lies with the family, and therefore it is imperative that every person who works in the setting does so in partnership with parents to ensure that the child's rights are protected.

Care is the foundation of the work of all ELC settings. Ensuring that those who work in the setting constantly bear that in mind is underpinned by the quality of the supervision processes in the setting. The supervisor should emphasise this focus as well as reinforcing reflective practices through careful probing, exploring issues and providing support. Actions taken should be based on reflection and the impact on the children, their parents/guardians and all stakeholders. Ensuring that children are cared for and learn in ways that suit their stage of development is a joint enterprise involving all in the setting.

Enabling and supporting supervisees in turn enables them to understand the importance of such partnership approaches, which are central to good ELC setting organisation. This is never more obvious than when a child has an Access and Inclusion Model (AIM) classification. An AIM specifies additional structures to support that particular child to participate fully in a partnership approach to their needs and the assessment produced for them. Those supports may require the supervisor to engage with outside agencies to ensure that the child's needs are met and they may need to take a collaborative approach in their dealings with other agencies. Everybody is working to help the child reach their potential and engage meaningfully in the care and learning in the ELC setting. It is the duty of the supervisor to engage with the provision of the additional supports and to educate all staff on the method of implementation of the suggested supports for that individual child.

MEETING REGULATORY AND LEGISLATIVE REQUIREMENTS

From the moment an ELC setting is planned, the owner/operator must engage in ensuring that every aspect of the proposed setting meets with the Child Care Act (Early Years Services) Regulations 2016. These requirements demand standards of compliance in every aspect of the workings of an ELC. Every supervisor must ensure that their setting meets the standards required all the time.

Organising the environment, keeping it safe and secure, and vetting staff, volunteers and visitors is the responsibility of the supervisor. Dealing with complaints, data protection issues and procedures, fire drills, food safety, hygiene, health, risk assessment, insurance, human resources and much more also fall within their remit. Oversight and the ability to envisage and offset any potential problem requires them to be vigilant, informed and aware of every aspect of the operation of the ELC setting and the work of those within it.

Mandatory reporting of suspicions or incidents of child abuse or concerns for the wellbeing of a child requires a supervisor to ensure that such suspicions or evidence are recorded, reported and followed through. Knowing each child and the impact of incidents that have happened to them can be upsetting when they arise in supervision sessions. Maturity, resilience and courage in such situations are the hallmarks of a good supervisor, as is the emotional maturity to be aware of supports needed by supervisees.

THINK AND REFLECT

Think about other regulatory responsibilities the Child Care Act 1991 (Early Years Services) Regulations 2016 place on supervisors and examine what qualities are required of a good supervisor to meet those responsibilities. (For example, fire safety, inspections ...).

MANAGING FUNDING AND SUSTAINABILITY

While the owner/operator is ultimately responsible for ensuring compliance with the registration and oversight of an ELC setting, it is usually the supervisor who deals with potential funding issues and their day-to-day, month-to-month management procedures inform the actual funding process. This is done by the owner/operator and the supervisor ensuring that application processes are correct, recorded and updated.

Funding, when obtained, needs to be allocated as laid out in the budget that informed the application. ECCE funding and returns, AIM supports, returns and implementation of those supports and their constant oversight are in the remit of the supervisor. Costs are a constant focus for a supervisor in the ongoing work of an ELC setting. Organising funding for activities and excursions, CPD for staff, and holiday relief staff require particular skills, and the supervisor needs to have the management and financial acumen to ensure that the setting is fully functioning and sustainable.

SELF-AWARENESS AND CAPACITY BUILDING

Every supervisor supports others as part of their job. They need inner strength and self-awareness and at the same time they need to be aware of the needs, strengths and challenges of others.

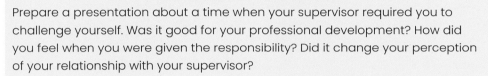

THINK AND REFLECT

Prepare a presentation about a time when your supervisor required you to challenge yourself. Was it good for your professional development? How did you feel when you were given the responsibility? Did it change your perception of your relationship with your supervisor?

Supervisors bear a responsibility for staff, children, parents/guardians, workers, volunteers, the community, the owners/operators, and for their own wellbeing. The supervisor cannot micro-manage but must build informed and informing procedures throughout their work to build capacity from within the setting. Building relationships is important for every supervisor and creating a supportive environment is what ensures that this is sustained for the betterment of every stakeholder in the ELC setting.

Integrity, honesty, openness, insight, responsibility, keeping themselves informed and being aware of their own self-care ensures that the supervisor can engage dynamically with the challenges they face every day. But they should also be aware of their own limitations, mindful of their own fragility and their own needs.

THINK AND REFLECT

As a group, invite a supervisor from an ELC setting (preferably one where nobody in the group is on professional placement) and have a conversation about the skills they feel are necessary for supervisors to have. Create a poster based on what you feel are the most important parts of that conversation.

You will realise by now the multiplicity of skills (both hard skills and transversal skills) that great supervisors have. Make a list of the ones mentioned in this chapter, pick ten and investigate how you feel you might develop those skills as part of your development as a professional ECL practitioner.

Most practitioners, wherever they are on their professional journey, can learn a lot from others. In an ELC setting the structures that support the care and learning of all staff also ensure that the teams that work within each setting have opportunities to expand their range of achievements and skills with the assistance of good supervisors and good supervision practices.

Team building and team supports are fundamental to the running, support and development of every ELC setting and will be discussed in the next chapter.

Recap

1. **List some of the considerations that arise when a CPD plan is being developed for staff.**

2. **Name some limitations which can arise in relation to CPD plans for a setting.**

3. **Write a blog post about the strengths of good supervisors.**

4. **Using your blog post, design a job advertisement for an ELC supervisor in your setting.**

References and further reading

Amabile, T. and Kramer, S. (2011) 'The power of small wins', *Harvard Business Review*, May, 71–80

Hollander, E. and Offerman, L. (1990) 'Power and leadership in organizations', *American Psychology* 45 (February): 179–89

McPartland, E. (2012) *Supervision and Leadership in Childcare*. Dublin: Gill & Macmillan

Building and Supporting Teams in ELC Settings

8

Learning Goals

In this chapter, learners will:

* Learn about teams, team dynamics and how to identify a team

* Learn about the stages of teams

* Examine the individual roles in teams

Introduction

If you have completed one or more of your work placements or practicums in ELC settings you will be familiar with the different developmental stages used to classify the rooms that children are placed in during the day – wobbler, toddler, pre-school, etc. People who work in those rooms operate in teams, and each of those teams is embedded in the overall team that is the ELC setting.

Supervisors work with supervisees who are at different stages on the continuum towards being competent and professional practitioners. This requires them to embed supervision on both an individual and a team basis. When you work in a team, that team becomes part of your identity as a professional practitioner.

Effective, enabling and supportive work settings are enabling organisations where management are aware of the need to support all team members and the outcomes are better for everybody. In ELC settings the biggest winner when teams work well together is the children who are being cared for by those teams. A positive atmosphere emanates from such settings and effort can be concentrated where it needs to be – on the children within each team's care and support. There is therefore a win–win for everyone in the setting when teams are properly managed and supported.

What is a team?

A team is a combination of more than one person who work together, co-ordinating their effort towards a final outcome, and who describe themselves as being part of a particular unit.

* A team consists of more than one person.

* The people in the team work together.

* They also co-ordinate their efforts to reach a shared goal or outcome.

* They see themselves as working as part of a unit or team.

THINK AND REFLECT

Look at the following example of groups of people and evaluate whether they meet these criteria. Which are teams and which are not?

* Six people at a bus stop

* A demonstration attended by 100 people

* Two thousand people at a concert

* Five staff members in the toddler room

Using a well-known but anonymous example from business management writing, a good way to understand the concept of the interwoven nature of teams is by looking at geese.

LESSONS FROM GEESE

Fact 1:

As geese fly they flap their wings, which produces an 'uplift' for the birds that follow, and they fly in a V shape, which increases by 71% the distance each bird could fly alone.

Lesson: People who share a common direction and sense of community can get where they are going quicker when they help each other.

Fact 2:

When a goose falls out of the formation, it feels the drag and resistance of flying alone and quickly moves back into formation to take advantage of the lifting power of the bird immediately in front of it.

Lesson: It makes sense for us to stay with those heading in our direction and we should be willing to accept help from others and give help to others.

Fact 3:

When the goose at the front of the V gets tired it goes to the back of the V formation and another goose takes up the lead position.

Lesson: It pays to take turns doing the hard work and sharing the leadership role. People depend on each other's skills and abilities at different times and benefit from sharing.

Fact 4:

The geese flying in formation honk to encourage everyone to keep up the uniform speed of the group.

Lesson: Encouragement in groups leads to a better outcome.

Fact 5:

When a goose gets sick or is wounded or shot down, two other geese drop out of the formation to support the goose and protect it. They stay with it until the goose dies or is fit to resume the flight after which they rejoin the original V or create a new formation.

Lesson: If we are clever we will stand by each other in difficult times as well as when we are not challenged as that helps us to regenerate.

Adapted from Organisational Development Network 1991 (author unknown)

People may describe themselves as a team but if one (or more) of the above criteria is missing, they are not a team. In sport there are sometimes occasions when the team just did not work together and for each other and were unsuccessful as a result.

The lesson from geese explains what needs to be incorporated into the work of the team in order to ensure that a team is effective:

* Teams need to include all members in some way, although each may have different roles and responsibilities.

* There needs to be a shared objective that drives the work of the team and they must all know what is required of them.

* Work organisation may be the central aspect of teams working effectively.

* Putting the interests of the team before self-interest is required to get the job of the team done.

* Sometimes members of the team need help from other members of the team. When they provide that support everybody wins.

* Sometimes the team needs to be reformed.

Team dynamics

Successful team dynamics might look something like the diagram in Figure 8.1.

Figure 8.1 Factors that contribute to team dynamics (McPartland 2012)

In ELC settings, it is the supervisor who is responsible for the effectiveness of teams. They initiate the formation of the team, observe its performance, provides its shared focus and assist the members to get the support they need as well as providing ongoing focus on the outcome/goal of the team. In order to do this the supervisor needs to understand the dynamics of teams.

How teams happen

There are several ways in which teams can arise:

* **Formed teams** may be created for a situation where they have a shared responsibility. For example, in a baby room or a toddler room the team may be formed because there needs to be a team in each room who will work together to work with children at those specific stages in their development and the team members are chosen because they have the relevant skills.

* **Organic teams** are created when a specific job needs to be done. The team members have the skills required to do that job.

* **Orchestrated teams** are created by a person in charge putting people together in positions or circumstances where they are likely to form a team. This may be because they all have a particular qualification or a specific skill and it would be natural to expect that they would form an alliance.

Stages of teams

Bruce Tuckman, acknowledged as an authority on teams, examined the processes of team formation and development. He analysed the reasons why teams can be challenging when they are first formed and may take a while to really get to work together (Tuckman 1965; Tuckman & Jensen 1977). According to Tuckman, teams go through the following stages:

* **Forming:** when teams start to get to know each other. The supervisor's role at this stage is to assist members to explore how the team will work. They will create opportunities for each member to get to know the other members, for example ice-breaker exercises.

* **Storming:** when people learn a little more about each other and start to become comfortable but do not yet quite know each other's boundaries. This can lead to issues of power dynamics, conflict, disagreements and there is a period when the team lacks unity and can recognise that themselves.

* **Norming:** when the individual boundaries are understood and people in the team begin to accept each other's individual preferences, ways of being and particular personalities. Team members feel that things are settling down and they can move on towards the goal. The supervisor will set out expectations for each member, support them to communicate effectively together and accept the development of shared values and ways of working.

* **Performing:** where the focus of everyone in the team is on getting the task done and understanding the most effective ways of achieving their goal. The supervisor should at this stage have moved to managing the way the job gets done and ensuring that it fits with the values and expectations of the setting, but it is up to the team to do the job.

* **Adjourning:** when the task of the team has been completed or the team is being discontinued. This stage is usually marked by some sort of debriefing, which the supervisor oversees. People acknowledge that the task has been done or the goal achieved and celebrate the end of the process.

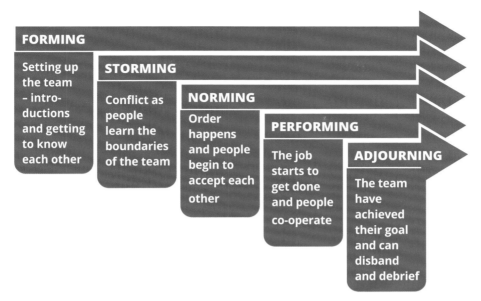

Figure 8.2 Tuckman's team stages

There is not always a clear pathway through the team building process. For instance, staff members may change responsibilities in the setting, leading to an adjustment of their place or the perception of their place in the team. Teams do not always move seamlessly from forming to storming to norming and then on to performing; they may well go back and forth from one level to another – forming could be revisited as a member changes, for instance.

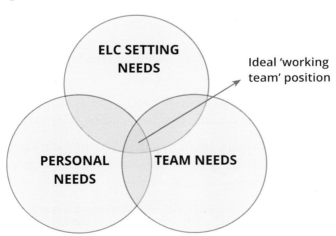

Figure 8.3 Finding the ideal team structure

A team within an ELC setting – room members, for example – are also a part of the overall team of the ELC so there can be knock-on effects of changes in a team. There is a dynamic to the process that needs to be overseen and supported as it changes over time. Focus must be on the overall values and mission of the ELC setting itself, but within that there needs to be a supported process to align personal positions, team positions and setting positions, as shown in Figure 8.3. When these are aligned the team will reach its best potential.

What is required of the supervisor at all stages is to understand and support the team members to realise that they will go through different stages in their working relationships. While the transition from forming to performing might well be quick and easy, there is no guarantee that it will not be problematic and protracted.

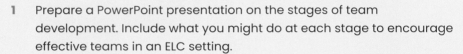

THINK AND REFLECT

1   Prepare a PowerPoint presentation on the stages of team development. Include what you might do at each stage to encourage effective teams in an ELC setting.

2   Draw a cartoon which depicts the stages of team development. Use facial expressions to show how you think the team members might feel at each stage.

Team behaviours

Understanding how teams work helps a supervisor to work with team members in supervision and to support a supervisee to analyse their position and team behaviour or role and how they think their contribution is helping the team or how they might like or need to alter their approach within the team.

Robert Baron (1986) said that there are two distinct aspects to the success of team behaviours that help teams achieve:

*   **Task specialism behaviours** – generating ideas, giving opinions, researching possibilities, pulling the possibilities together and energising the team.

*   **Socio-emotional behaviours** – encouraging, pulling the team together, reducing tension, following up on what needs to be done to make something happen, and compromise so that tensions can be eliminated.

Meredith Belbin (1993) identified nine distinct roles that team members can play and categorised them into three aspects, as shown in the table below.

Belbin's classification of team roles

Role grouping	Role labels	Actions and contributions
Action-oriented	Shaper	Challenges the team to improve
	Implementer	Puts ideas into action
	Completer/finisher	Ensures thorough and timely completion of task
People-oriented	Co-ordinator	Acts as chairperson and people organiser
	Team worker	Encourages co-operation and joint work
	Resource investigator	Explores opportunities that can help the team
Thought-oriented	Plant	Presents new ideas and approaches that could be used
	Monitor/evaluator	Studies and analyses the options that are presented
	Specialist	Provides specialist skills or knowledge that can help the consideration of options

Belbin's categories have become well known and, while it might be possible in the modern technological world to adjust some of these categories, they can help people to understand their own strengths and challenges in team environments. They can thus facilitate discussions in supervision sessions that can ensure that teamwork is embedded, understood and supported in all ELC settings.

Extend Your Learning

 Go to YouTube, search for and watch:

* 'Belbin's 9 Team Roles'
* 'How do Belbin's roles work in teams'

When you investigate Belbin's work and categorisation of team roles and behaviours it might be easy to imagine yourself as fitting into one particular category, but this may not be your best role. This can be explored within supervision. Such discussions will help a supervisee to understand that in different teams with different purposes they may well embrace different roles – they are not finite – and they may even change role as they develop within the team.

Look at your class group and how they interact when given group projects to undertake as part of your training. Can you list which class members you think are:

* Implementers

* Resource investigators

* Shapers

* Finishers?

Now consider this scenario. The class has asked you to organise an invitation for the Minister for Children, Equality, Disability, Integration and Youth to visit your college.

Who do you think would be the best specialists and co-ordinators to assist you in this task?

Are they the same in each instance?

Team conflict

Conflict is often (but not exclusively) the primary concern at the storming stage and it can affect everybody in the team. From a supervision point of view, conflict needs to be understood and mitigated in order to settle the team and enable them to move on with the task at hand. The supervisor needs to realise and explain what is happening and to support all team members. This is especially important in ELC settings where the main focus is on the children's care and wellbeing. Conflict has the potential for contagion, so it needs to be resolved. A cohesive team will be good role models for the children.

Conflict is most likely to occur in teams where there are different personalities, positions, understandings and interests. Some conflicts can be beneficial in getting the work of the team done. However, conflict that interferes with the natural ebb and flow of a team working in a cohesive manner can be harmful and it is therefore necessary to find a compromise between the conflicting positions (Mullins 2007). If there is no conflict at all, a team can become stuck in 'group think', continuing to do things in the same way over and over again without exploring other ways that might prove more efficient or effective.

Karen Jehn (1997) identified two basic types of conflict that arise in teamwork: task-oriented conflict and relationship conflict.

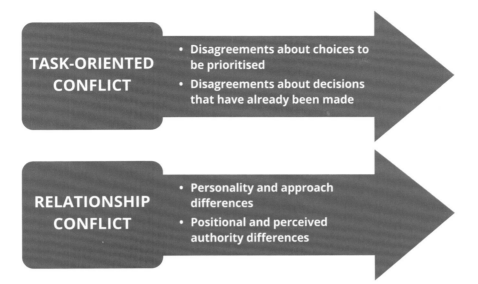

Figure 8.4 Jehn's conflict types

Finding solutions to conflict is important as time, effort and success can be a hostage to conflict. Some level of conflict can be healthy – if carefully managed it can serve to change positions for the better – but where the level of conflict in a team is proving harmful either to team members individually or to the team as a whole, it is imperative that it is mediated before it spirals out of control and interferes with the whole concept of teamwork in the setting.

STYLES OF CONFLICT MANAGEMENT WITHIN TEAMS

Whatever the cause of conflict there are several styles of conflict management that can be employed. They each have different outcomes, which may impact on the team dynamic:

* **Dominate:** Assertive – do it my way. This may be necessary when the issue demands an immediate response and there are risks in not doing the task as directed (e.g. fire drill procedures).

* **Avoid:** Non-assertive. Doing nothing and seeing how the situation works out may be appropriate.

* **Compromise:** A moderate amount of intervention. Both sides agree to differ and make the necessary adjustments to get the task done.

* **Accommodate:** People realise that they must move on. The goal is more important than the conflict and they are willing to see the other side of the issue.

* **Collaborate:** There may be a need to negotiate or bargain about the best option for a solution to the conflict and both sides want a resolution to be found.

It is important to realise that the team themselves may direct which style is best for them and the situations or tasks they are involved in. The supervisor may not need to intervene immediately but supporting the team members to understand their own position can result in a growth process within the team. This will facilitate the team to move on to the next stage of development but with a realisation and understanding of the processes to ensure that task focus is maintained.

Additionally, good team dynamics save on resources, including the time of the supervisor and of individual team members whose focus should be on the work that needs to be done.

THINK AND REFLECT

Think about teams you have been a part of and conflicts that arose in those team situations. Were you able to deal with the conflict on your own? If so, what helped you resolve the conflict? Has the experience changed how you would work in a team now?

STRATEGIES FOR RESOLVING CONFLICT

While teams often resolve their own differences, a supervisor might have to deal with persistent conflict. This can involve the six-step process of resolving issues in the setting (Ly 2018):

1. Define the source of the problem and explore how or why it has provoked the conflict.

2. Look beyond the incident to see if something that has changed recently has contributed to the conflict.

3. Request solutions – ask those involved in the conflict if they can suggest solutions so that they feel an ownership of the resolving action.

4. Think about barriers to the solutions that are suggested and see how those barriers might be overcome.

5. Identify the solution that all those involved in the conflict can agree on and support.

6. Agreement should be obtained by everyone involved and there should be recognition of how it will be monitored in the future.

What is really important is that fairness, equity, agreement and support are facilitated in any process of conflict resolution as this ensures that people buy in to the solutions arrived at and feel that they are supported, understood and valued in the process. The steps outlined above do not automatically lead to resolution; because to work they need 'buy-in' from everyone involved in the dispute. The solutions might involve people changing their own positions, which is not an immediate process – indeed, it is often more effective if time is allowed for the process. However, in such situations time is not limitless, and it can help if the supervisor draws up a framework for the team to follow.

Recap

1. **Create a template for team tasks that could be used in your setting so that people's skills can best be utilised in new tasks that need to be completed.**

2. **Name the five stages of teams as outlined by Tuckman (1965).**

3. **Name five stages of conflict management in teams.**

References and further reading

Baron, R. (1986) *Behavior in Organizations* (2nd edn). Boston MA: Allyn & Bacon

Belbin, M. (1993) *Team Roles at Work*. Oxford: Butterworth Heinemann

Jehn, K. (1997) 'A quantitative analysis of conflict types and dimensions in organizational groups', *Administrative Science Quarterly* 42: 530–57

Ly, C. (2018) 'The emotional backpack: managing conflict resolution with children of trauma', *HighScope Journal for Early Educators* Vol 2: Number 2. Fall

McPartland, E. (2012) *Supervision and Leadership in Childcare*. Dublin: Gill & Macmillan

Mullins, I. (2007) *Management and Organisational Behaviour* (8th edn). Harlow: Prentice Hall

Tuckman, B. (1965) 'Development sequence in small groups', *Psychological Bulletin* 63: 384–99

Tuckman, B. and Jensen, M. (1977) 'Stages of small group development revisited', *Group and Organizational Studies* 2: 419–27

Qualification Developments in ELC in Ireland

9

Learning Goals

In this chapter, learners will:

* Learn the different approaches to role categorisations in ELC and how they impact on qualification requirements

* Learn about the four As of competency

* Learn about the CoRe project, and the CoRe dimensions of quality, and its implications for the professionalisation of ELC

Introduction

People are at the heart of every ELC setting. They support the children in the setting, observe and support their development, introduce education and learning to each child according to their developmental stage and provide the supports that may be identified for any or every child in the setting. They are also the people who introduce children to challenges, fun, knowledge and experiences that will sustain each child's holistic development for years after their direct intervention in their lives. Ensuring that the right people are on the team is an important aspect of every supervisor's job.

We saw in Chapter 8 how important it is to get the right team in place. It is also important to ensure that staff are well qualified and trained to work in the ELC setting so that the children in their care receive the best possible experience at the beginning of each child's lifelong learning journey.

Occupational roles in ELC

Ireland has developed its childcare and education sector more slowly than some other European countries. It has been led by the international concept of education levels i.e. distinguishing between different levels in the ELC sector, which has been the subject of much consideration for many years.

It is important to note the journey which Ireland has taken in raising the provision and profile of childcare and early education for our most vulnerable citizens who will in time become our decision-makers and the custodians of our next generations. This journey is one that aims to raise the profile of those who work in the sector from a best-fit, cheap and undervalued system to 'a competent system' (Urban *et al.* 2012) of educated, educating and professional practitioners. It is interesting to follow the ebb and flow of developments and research in Ireland and how that reflects and is informed by wider European research and development.

Steps towards a model framework for qualifications

In 2002 the *Model Framework for Education, Training and Professional Development in the Early Childhood Care and Education Sector* began the process of classifying those working in what has now become known as the ECL sector. The Model Framework was designed to allow those working in the sector (then known as the early childhood education and care (ECEC) sector) 'to identify clearly where they are located in terms of their own professional development' (DJELR 2002). The proposed categorisation of practitioner in that report, which were 'agreed as working titles by the sector', was:

* Basic practitioner

* Intermediate practitioner

* Experienced practitioner

* Advanced practitioner

* Expert practitioner

This classification of roles is somewhat mirrored by those outlined in the European Commission's ET2020 Working Group (European Commission 2021), which defines them as:

Core practitioner: An individual with pedagogic training who leads practice for a group of children at the class or playroom level and works directly with children and their families. They may also be called pedagogues, educators, pedagogical staff, pre-school, pre-primary, kindergarten or early childhood teachers.

Assistant (not in every country): Works alongside the core practitioner with a group of children or class on a daily basis and usually meet lower qualification levels than core practitioners.

Head of centre-based ECEC setting (leader): May be responsible for monitoring children, supervising other staff, contact with parents and guardians, and/or planning, preparing and carrying out the pedagogical work in the centre.

Professional role: A professional role is regulated and requires the individual to develop and reflect on their own practice and, with parents and children, create a learning environment which is constantly renewed and improved. They are expected to take responsibility for high quality in the ECEC service.

Professional leadership: This position requires skills, behaviours and competencies related to supporting children's care and education, pedagogy, engagement with parents, the local community, staff management and organisation.

Adapted from ET2020 Working Group (European Commission 2021)

The Model Framework report (DJELR, 2002) also focused on how practitioners would advance along the continuum of roles. It envisaged:

basic practitioner

↓

intermediate practitioner

↓

experienced practitioner

↓

advanced practitioner

↓

expert practitioner.

This progress would be supported internally by providing experience and training or externally by sourcing educational advancement. A set of core values would highlight essential knowledge areas that would guide the practitioner's progress through the levels of competency.

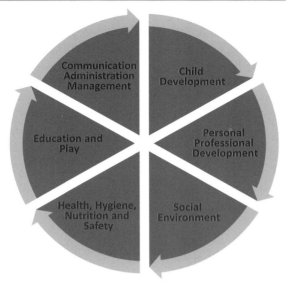

Figure 9.1 Competency progression path

Progress through the levels of competency would be through the four As:

* Awareness

* Acquisition

* Application

* Assessment and extension

Early Childhood Care and Education Scheme 2010

The 2002 report has since been distilled a little with the establishment of the Early Childhood Care and Education (ECCE) plan, a government-supported scheme to provide one free year (now extended to two years) of pre-school care. The ECCE scheme provided that as part of the ECCE funding, levels of training qualifications would determine the responsibilities of workers in ECCE and that the minimum qualification for people working directly with children would be a QQI Level 5 major award in ECCE. There would be different funding available for settings that employed practitioners with additional training or qualifications:

Major Award QQI Level 5   Childcare worker

Major Award QQI Level 6   Room leader for ECCE

Major Award QQI Level 7   Room leader – higher capitation rate

Major Award QQI Level 8   Operator

Terminology and qualifications

Some confusion about childcare provision has resulted from Ireland's approach to the ECCE sector. That provision relates to children directly before they begin school (at age 5), and have reached, initially, age 4 (one-year provision) and now age 3 (two-year provision). ECCE falls within the wider aspect of what is recognised throughout Europe as early childhood education and care (ECEC). ECEC, then, refers to Europe-wide provision for children from *birth to school age*. In Ireland ECCE falls within the European categorisation but it does not have as wide a remit as ECEC.

Figure 9.2 ECCE is embedded in ECEC

Ireland's ECCE approach was revisited in 2017 in the *Review of Occupational Role Profiles in Ireland in Early Childhood Education and Care* (Urban *et al.* 2017). This report observed that in Ireland there had 'been two decades of unprecedented efforts to develop, expand and sustain better quality for children and families in a highly fragmented sector with a multitude of actors following diverse practice and policy agendas, and pursuing often contradictory interests' (Urban et al, 2017, p. 10). The review reflected the conclusion in a report by the Organisation for Economic Co-operation and Development (OECD) that 'significant energies and funding will need to be invested in the field to create a system in tune with the needs of a full employment economy and with new understandings of how young people develop and learn' (OECD 2014).

The CoRe Project

The CoRe Project was an international research project, funded by the European Commission, that examined competency requirements in ECEC (Urban *et al.*, 2012). This study looked at the concept of competency and professionalism in early childhood practice and examined the concept within the relationship of quality and professionalisation. The concept of quality in the CoRe report was considered to be a multi-dimensional concept with at least five dimensions, as shown in Figure 9.3.

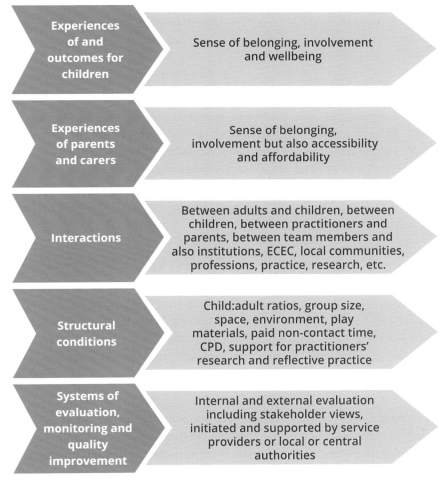

Experiences of and outcomes for children	Sense of belonging, involvement and wellbeing
Experiences of parents and carers	Sense of belonging, involvement but also accessibility and affordability
Interactions	Between adults and children, between children, between practitioners and parents, between team members and also institutions, ECEC, local communities, professions, practice, research, etc.
Structural conditions	Child:adult ratios, group size, space, environment, play materials, paid non-contact time, CPD, support for practitioners' research and reflective practice
Systems of evaluation, monitoring and quality improvement	Internal and external evaluation including stakeholder views, initiated and supported by service providers or local or central authorities

Figure 9.3 The five CoRe dimensions of quality

CoRe used the generic title 'practitioner' rather than the diversity of titles used in the ECEC sector in different European countries. CoRe also referred to the 'transformative potential of professional practice which is constantly co-constructed, de-constructed and reconstructed in the relationships with children, families and local communities'. In using the generic term 'practitioner education' it allowed for:

* **Initial professional preparation:** Qualifying or non-qualifying professionalising routes undertaken before being involved in practice
* **Continuing professional development:** In-service courses, team supervision, tutoring, pedagogical guidance, counselling, etc.

Hmelak notes the continual and rapid development and change in the ECEC sector and points out that professionals have to constantly adjust to their multifaceted roles in caring and educating young children, suggesting that this is only possible with a solidly educated and innovative workforce that regularly upgrades and improves its knowledge (Hmelak 2010, quoted in Urban *et al.* 2017). This reflects the CoRe approach to professional education as developmental in nature.

The Learner Fund (2014)

The Learner Fund was set up in 2014 to support the upskilling of educators, especially in the ECCE sector. It initially provided funding to enable upskilling to achieve QQI Level 5 and Level 6 major awards and since 2017 it has provided limited retrospective financial funding up to €750 for educators completing QQI Level 7 and Level 8 awards (provided they did not receive funding from elsewhere). The training fund has supported more than 2,750 learners at Levels 7 and 8 and 4,400 at Levels 5 and 6.

Ireland's Indecon Report (2021)

Ireland is constantly reviewing its approaches in relation to European ECEC. There is an awareness that Ireland's system needs to move towards a cohesive recognition within those European structures. It is reasonable to assume that funding initiatives will be more streamlined if Ireland does adjust its approach and makes the sector more comparable to those in other EU counties, since European unity as a concept envisages uniformity of identity, funding and approaches.

There is an increasing awareness that the ELC and school-age childcare (SAC) models, which operate separately, need to be combined in order to ensure that funding and uniformity of service is obtained for all children from birth to 6 years. This brings with it challenges to the goal of having uniform qualification requirements throughout the sector, as many childminders working outside ECCE have not thus far been required to have qualifications at the level of ECCE practitioners.

Acknowledging the commitment within *First 5: A Whole of Government Strategy for Babies, Young Children and their Families*, published in 2018, the Indecon Review in 2021 emphasised the need for services, funding and provisions for both ELC and SAC to be more co-ordinated and for a cohesive proposal to be developed to align qualification levels across both provisions combined (Indecon, 2021). The funding model and procedures will be aligned and streamlined to meet the government's commitments under First 5 and training funds will be committed to that vision.

FIRST 5 COMMITMENT

First 5 states a number or goals for the ELC sector and those who work and will work within it:

> " Those working with babies, young children and their families are at the very heart of the early childhood system. There are central to delivering high-quality services, and play a crucial role in bringing about the changes necessary to realising the vision for early childhood. "

(Government of Ireland 2018, p.110)

To bring that plan to fruition it commits to developing:

> " A Workforce Development Plan to ensure the appropriate number of early learning and care and school-age childcare staff at all levels in the sector. The Workforce Development Plan will support the achievement of the above targets [for a graduate-led workforce and for minimum qualifications for childminders and school-age children]. The Workforce Development Plan will also set out plans to raise the profile of careers in early learning and care and school-age childcare, establish a career framework and leadership development opportunities and will work towards building a more gender-balanced and diverse workforce. Consideration will also be given to broader early learning and care and school-age childcare workforce, including those in inspection, monitoring and training roles and support those who facilitate practice placements. "

(Government of Ireland 2018, p. 110)

The commitments in First 5 led to the Workforce Plan 2022–2028 and can be clearly seen as focused on combining the elements of ECCE and SAC within the ECEC umbrella. This will have the effect of creating a more comprehensive and cohesive sector for everyone but more especially for all the children of Ireland.

The Workforce Plan 2022–2028

The most recently published *Nurturing Skills: The Workforce Plan for Early Learning and Care and School-Age Childcare, 2022– 2028* (Government of Ireland 2022) envisages the development of the workforce under five distinct pillars:

* **Pillar 1** Establishing a career framework

* **Pillar 2** Raising qualification levels

* **Pillar 3** Developing a national CPD system

* **Pillar 4** Supporting recruitment, retention and diversity

* **Pillar 5** Moving towards regulation of the progression

The Workforce Plan examines the process outlined in the Indecon review and sets out a vision for the combination of ELC and SAC providers' qualifications by 2028:

1. Continuation of QQI Level 5 as the minimum requirement for ELC, but with a target of increasing the proportion of Early Years Educators who have a QQI Level 6 (or higher) qualification from 72% in 2021 to 85% by 2028. Because there is no specific SAC-focused QQI Level 5 award it is proposed to work on a combined Level 5 programme and to expand it to update Levels 5 upwards in combined format going forward.

2. A target (but not a regulatory requirement) that all Lead Educators should have a QQI Level 7 (or higher) qualification by 2028, up from 43% in 2021. Continue to monitor progress towards achieving the target and consider alternative measures that may be needed to ensure the target is met.

3. All managers (persons in charge) of ELC setting should by 2028 be required to have at least a QQI Level 6 qualification (96% already have this), with a target that managers should be qualified to QQI Level 7 (or higher). In addition a requirement that managers of SAC settings have a QQI Level 5 award by 2028.

4. Training in management skills specific to ELC and SAC settings will be developed and made available to all managers (both ELC and SAC).

5. Training and support will be further developed for managers and staff with leadership responsibilities that may be distributed across a setting, such as leadership in pedagogy, diversity and inclusion, family and community partnership, and student placement and induction. Additionally consideration will be given to the further development of identified roles of additional responsibility across a setting, building on the existing model of the Inclusion Co-ordinator established within AIM, which may include responsibility for mentoring and supporting co-professionals in the setting as an area of practice.

6. Work will begin during 2022–2028 on developing and incrementally introducing an induction process through research, consultation, piloting and review, along with actions to develop services' capacity and external supports for induction. This process will support movement towards a future requirement for all entrants into the profession (other than childminders) at all qualification levels to complete a supported induction period.

It is clear from these developments that there is work to be continued in ensuring that those who work in the ELC and SAC areas are properly prepared, supported and educated to do the work that will be required of them to fulfil the vision of First 5. For the children of Ireland and their parents/guardians this is something that ensures the best standard of care and governance that will support children's development and education.

Extend Your Learning

 Read Appendix 3 of the Workforce Plan for Early Learning and Care and School-Age Childcare, 2022–2028.

* How would you like to see your skills develop in light of the Role Profiles outlined?

* What training would you need to get to the level you would like to achieve?

THINK AND REFLECT

1 Create a timeline poster of the development of qualification requirements in Irish ELC to date. Display it in your room: it will help you to remember the key dates, reports and developmental steps in the process to get all ELC and SAC staff to a uniform level of qualification.

2 Write a short synopsis of the implications of qualifications on the journey to professionalism in the ELC sector.

Recap

1. **What is the basis of the CoRe project?**
2. **What are the Indecon report outcomes for ELC?**
3. **How do the CoRe elements support the *First 5* report?**

References and further reading

DJELR (Department of Justice, Equality and Law Reform) (2002) *Model Framework for Education, Training and Professional Development in the Early Childhood Care and Education Sector*. Dublin: Government Publications Office

European Commission (2021) *ET2020 Working Group Early Childhood Education and Care: Final Report*. Luxembourg: Publications Office of the European Union

Government of Ireland (2018) *First 5: A Government Strategy for Babies, Young Children and their Families, 2019–2028*. Dublin: Stationery Office

Government of Ireland (2022) *Nurturing Skills: The Workforce Plan for Early Learning and Care and School-Age Childcare, 2022–2028*. Dublin: Stationery Office <https://www.gov.ie/en/publication/97056-nurturing-skills-the-workforce-plan-for-early-learning-and-care-elc-and-school-age-childcare-sac-2022-2028>

Hmelak, M. (2010) 'Professional Development of Preschool Educators' in T. Janik and P. Knecht (eds), *New Pathways in the Professional Development of Teachers*. Berlin: LIT-Verlag

Indecon (2021) *Review of Early Learning and Care ('ELC') and School Age Childcare ('SAC') Operating Model in Ireland*. Dublin: Indecon International Consultants, for DCEDIY

OECD (2004) *Thematic Review of Early Childhood Education and Care Policy in Ireland*. Dublin: Stationery Office

Urban, M., Vandenbroeck, M., Van Laere, K., Lazzari, A. and Peeters, J. (2012) 'Towards competent systems in early childhood education and care: Implications for policy and practice', *European Journal of Education* 47(4): 508–26

Urban, M., Robson, S. and Scacchi, V. (2017) *Review of Occupational Role Profiles in Ireland in Early Childhood Education and Care*. London: Early Childhood Research Centre, University of Roehampton

10

Recruitment, Probation and Review in ELC

Learning Goals

In this chapter, learners will:

* Learn about the legal requirements for every ELC setting to have a recruitment policy

* Examine the reasons that such a recruitment policy is important

* Examine an outline of a recruitment process

* Learn about induction and probation processes in ELC

Introduction

This chapter will explore ways in which the right team can be recruited, the processes involved in selecting the right match of person to the setting and the legal requirements to support those selected as members of the team working in the ELC setting.

ELC recruitment policy

Under Regulation 9 of the Child Care Act 1991 (Early Years Services) Regulations 2016, settings are required to have a structure for management and to recruit appropriate people to ensure the quality and safety of the care given to children in the setting. Under Regulation 10 each setting must have a clear written policy and procedure in place which covers paid and unpaid workers in the setting. This ensures good governance and protection for both employees and employers while also ensuring that people who work in the setting have the required skills to match their interactions with the children.

If a setting does not have a written policy on recruitment its registration can be withdrawn until one is produced.

Why have a recruitment policy?

Openness should be the focus of any recruitment policy and one which operates in the highly regulated ELC setting needs to encourage a level of openness that is exemplary in order to satisfy several considerations unique to ELC settings. While transparency is vitally important, is it also necessary to have a clear policy so that everyone is included in the process, not just paid employees but also volunteers, students and contactors carrying out work in the setting.

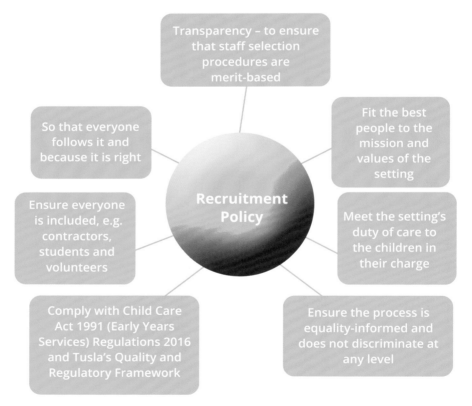

Figure 10.1 Reasons for having a written recruitment policy in ELC

When people engage in your recruitment process you need them to understand your needs and whether they feel they fit those needs. A recruitment drive is both expensive and time-consuming, so you want to know that those who do apply for the position are as near as possible to your ideal candidate for the job.

Much more importantly, a recruitment policy needs to carefully examine candidates (including identity checks before appointment) and to properly ensure that they are safe people to work with vulnerable young children. For this reason, every recruitment procedure must be complied with. Candidates must be Garda vetted, have two references and have undertaken Tusla training in child protection.

Complacency is never an option in the recruitment of ELC staff, students, volunteers or contractors.

Recruitment procedure

It is important that each step is followed in exactly the same manner for each candidate.

1. Look in detail at the competencies, qualifications and additional aspects which you want from the candidate to do the specific job you are offering. Look carefully at what is needed for the children in the setting and the stakeholders; the management needs; and the team needs.

2. Draw up a candidate booklet outlining the background, mission and values of the setting and a list of the competencies you identified at Step 1. The candidate booklet should also include a comprehensive job description, person specification, information on the terms and conditions of employment, a Garda vetting form and appropriate background information on the post.

3. Design an advertisement for the job and plan its dissemination, e.g. direct advertising, online listing or through an agency. Ensure that all advertisements and procedures are compliant with the Employment Equality Acts 1998 and 2004 and the Equal Status Acts 2000–2018. You must not discriminate against candidates based on race, religion, age, marital status, sexuality, gender, family status, disability or membership of the Travelling community.

4. The advertisement should emphasise that the successful candidate will require appropriate Garda/police vetting and written references in accordance with Children First.

5. Include a final date/time for applications to be received, a statement that canvassing will disqualify the candidate, and a schedule of when the interview and selection processes will be completed. Outline how candidates will be contacted and if interviews will be held in person or online. A timeline of the procedure is useful for everybody.

6. On receipt of the applications a shortlist should be drawn up of candidates whose details best fit the requirements outlined in the candidate handbook (for example, the candidate must have a QQI Level 5 at merit level and two years' post-qualification experience).

7. Convene an interview panel and draw up a core set of questions (interview protocol) which will ensure that all candidates are given a similar challenge at the interview. Allow for time to explore issues or potential challenges that might identify the best candidate. An independent observer is a good idea to verify that the interviews follow the agreed agenda and questions and that equal time is given to each interviewee.

8. Candidates should be given a date by which they will have a reply or feedback from the interview and whether there will be further shortlisting and a second round of interviews.

9. Following the final interview, the successful candidates should be given a provisional offer of employment. When identity checks, qualification certificate checks, successful Garda vetting, and confirmation and verification of two references (from the candidate's most recent employers) have been satisfied a formal offer of employment should be made.

THINK AND REFLECT

1   Research two job advertisements for supervisors in ELC settings. List the qualities, skills and experience and any special requirements that are requested. Do you think you have the skills and experience already? If not, what would you need to do to achieve them? From your analysis, work out a plan for your own development, including short- and long-term goals. Begin by acknowledging your current level of readiness for work in the ELC sector.

2   As a group, examine the two advertisements and plan (as if you were the interviewer) what questions you *as a group* would ask a prospective applicant at interview. Score the questions to develop an interview protocol for the jobs.

Confirming successful selection

Once you have decided on the ideal interviewee for the job and have informed them that they have been successful you can start to go through the identification and verification procedures:

* Check the person's identity (request two forms of identity) and confirm contact details, address, etc. Identity should be statutory documentation (e.g. a passport, driver's licence, public services card or ID card), which gives their full name, address, signature and photograph. A copy of the ID must be kept on file.

* Ensure they have the requisite visas to work in Ireland, if applicable.

* Verify that the person holds the qualifications they say they have.

* Contact the referees and ascertain that the reference presented is valid, proportionate and accurate.

* Organise a medical assessment (if that has been specified as a requirement for the job).

* Complete Garda vetting and verify that the person has no convictions that would make them unsuitable to work with children.

* Confirm the offer of employment to the new employee and agree a start date.

* Arrange for a pre-start visit to meet the team and discuss any arrangements that might be necessary, e.g. if the person needs assistance or has additional needs that must be met.

* Give the new employee an employment contract which outlines their terms and conditions (including any probation period) and addressing legal issues in relation to their employment (see Chapter 11).

* A 'Day 5 Statement' under the Employment (Miscellaneous Provision) Act 2018 (see Chapter 11) should be given within five days of the employee finding out that they have been successful.

Induction of new employees

'Tús maith leath na hoibre' – 'A good start is half the work' – is true of a good induction process for anyone starting in a new job, but especially so in an ELC setting.

If you can put yourself in the shoes of a new recruit you will realise how much detail they need to take in at induction and you can plan accordingly. An induction should take place for all new staff, students, volunteers and contractors in the setting. Specifics can change in relation to the position the inductee has (e.g. staff or volunteer), but following a carefully developed process ensures that all are equally informed about their position and their contribution to the team that is the complete ELC setting.

The new inductee should understand the fundamental ethos of the setting and the frameworks that apply to all work in the setting, such as Síolta and Aistear, and the pedagogical approaches the setting embraces.

If a buddy system is used, the inductee should be introduced to the buddy and should be told how it is envisaged they will support them, for how long, what procedures will be used for contact with the buddy, and the frequency of meetings with the buddy, if necessary.

The following should be considered in the development of any induction programme:

* All inductees should be met immediately on arrival, shown the cloakroom or staff room and where the toilets and kitchen are, and be provided with door codes, etc.

* Hours of work and break times or how they are allocated should be explained.

* Telephone usage and ICT security policies should be explained as soon as the inductee starts.

* A tour of the whole setting should take place, particularly if this is the first time the inductee has visited the setting.

* There should be a timetable and written outline of the induction process so that there is ample time for everything to be introduced and explained to the inductee.

* Every inductee should be given a copy of the setting's staff handbook which clearly outlines the code of conduct for staff and the setting's ethics statement.

* A hierarchical introduction to all staff and their responsibilities in the setting should be made. This could be done in pictorial format to make it easier for the new recruit to remember who everyone is and what they do. (Think about being introduced to a group of ten people and trying to remember later who does what and what their names were and this will guide your attention to this task.)

* A copy of all the policies and procedures of the setting should be provided and the inductee should be given time to read, study and, if necessary, ask questions. New inductees must sign that they have read and understood the policies and procedures. Understanding is the most important thing to achieve and should not be assumed. You could use a quiz or multiple choice test to check understanding.

* While you may have outlined in your job specification that staff should have completed the Tusla e-learning programme on Children First you may require them to update their certificate by re-doing the training as part of their induction. In any case, the inductee should be familiarised with the individual setting's child protection policy and its drop-off and collection procedures.

* The safety statement must also be read, studied and a signature indicating understanding should be retained on the new staff member's personnel file.

* In relation to filing signatures and statements of understanding (health and safety, child protection, policies and procedures, etc.), there should be an outline of the GDPR requirements for data protection purposes and an outline of procedures to be followed in the event of a GDPR policy query.

* Fire and emergency procedures should be carefully explained to the inductee and it is good practice that an unannounced fire drill takes place within the timeline of induction.

* First aid procedures and the location of first aid boxes (and defibrillators if available) should be clearly outlined and new staff should undergo a refresher first aid course during their induction.

* Location maps of necessary equipment should be supplied.

* Introduction to supervision and arrangement of the supervision contract should be part of any induction process (this is not likely to be on the first day or even the first week).

This list of suggestions is not exhaustive and is unlikely to be completed in just one day. The full induction process may take serval weeks to complete.

The completed induction checklist should become part of the inductee's personnel file and should be retained in line with the setting's GDPR statement and retention policy.

THINK AND REFLECT

1 Below is a sample outline induction policy. Design your own policy, including a timetable (as illustrated), to demonstrate your understanding of the processes and important aspects of induction.

Name _____ Date of Commencement: _____

Room allocated to: _____

Room supervisor: _____

Induction item	Completion date	Signatures	Issues arising
DAY ONE Greeting Cloakroom, toilets and facilities tour, etc.			
WEEK ONE			
MONTH ONE			

2   Include a list of policies that should be given (tip: see the Child Care Act 1991 (Early Years Services) Regulations 2016 to complete this checklist).

Policy	Date read and understood	Signatures of inductee and supervisor	Issues arising
Policy 1 (include specifics)			
Policy 2			
Policy 3			

Probation

Employing new personnel in any organisation comes with uncertainty about the ability of the new recruit to be proficient at the job they are employed to do. This is why contracts of employment contain the requirement for satisfactory completion of a period of probation for employees before their position is confirmed as permanent.

The employer must set a reasonable length of time for the probation period to ensure that there is no potential for abuse of the process (e.g. a probation period of 12 months and the employee is let go after 11 months and told that they have failed the review). Most contracts have a provision that probationary periods, which do not currently have a maximum or minimum period specified in law (but likely to be six months from August 2022 – see below) can be extended at least once, but only for a specific time period (in the interests of fair procedures and equity). If an extension is allowed, this must be stated in the contract. Probation periods were traditionally set at 11 months as that avoids the 12-month period of employment required to qualify for the application of the unfair dismissal procedures. From August 2022, under an EU directive on transparent and predictable working conditions (Directive (EU) 2019/1152), Ireland is expected to set the maximum period of probation at six months.

A probationary period allows the employee to learn the procedures and working culture of the organisation. It also helps the employer to decide if they are the right person for the organisation and the job. For that reason, along with the expectation of fairness, reasonableness and equity, there is a requirement that regular reviews take place throughout the probationary period so that the employee knows how they are progressing, what they might need to do to improve their performance and what supports are available to them.

An employee who is dismissed during or after a probationary period may currently have redress under the Industrial Relations (Amendment) Act 2015, but this may be limited because of the length of time they have worked for the employer. This process is likely to be reviewed under EU Directive 2019/1152 and the detail of how it will be adjusted in Irish law is currently awaited. Another option is to make a claim under the Industrial Relations Act 1969 (as amended) or even under the Equal Status Acts. Either way, there are limits to the possibility of getting the job back and pragmatism might direct you to get another job.

> **THINK AND REFLECT**
>
> A new employee started in the wobbler room today. What immediate actions should the supervisor of the wobbler room take and what should he have in place for the new employee? Create a 'to do' list for the supervisor to remind him of what he needs to do.

Buddy system for new inductees

A buddy system is one which supports the induction process and helps with the settling in of new recruits. Buddies will have the attributes shown in Figure 10.2.

The buddy is not a manager or supervisor, but a go-to person who has agreed to assist the new recruit to settle in by providing introductions and inclusive conversations for somebody who is possibly nervous and apprehensive. They introduce the new recruit to the cultural nuances of the setting and support the new recruit to find their way around the systems that they need to learn about.

The buddy system is not a continual process but more a tapered process – it is very supportive in the initial stage; it does not create dependency on one person but facilitates and supports the new recruit to gradually become independent.

Figure 10.2 The attributes of a good buddy

Performance reviews/appraisals

There is a distinction between a review/appraisal and the processes of supervision outlined in earlier chapters of this book.

The process of **supervision** is based on encouraging reflective practice and supporting development as a professional in the ECL setting.

Reviews/appraisals are used to assess the employee's actual performance in the setting.

REVIEWS DURING PROBATION

Because the probation period is a finite length of time (as outlined in the setting's employment contract), and because making the employee's position permanent will be conditional on successful completion of the probation process, it is necessary to have regular reviews/appraisals during the probation period in the interests of fairness, equity and the right to fair procedures.

Within the provision for probation in the employee's contract it should make clear:

* How long the probationary period lasts

* Whether it can be extended

* In what circumstances it can be extended (e.g. if a probationer were on sick leave would the probation period be suspended?)

* Whether there can be an appeal if the probation period is brought to an end before the expected finish date and the probationer is not offered permanent employment. It should also be clear on what grounds, if any, such an appeal could be based.

How often such reviews take place may be dependent on the setting's internal procedures, but they should be appropriately spaced to allow the probationer to assess their feedback from each review/appraisal and adjust their approach if necessary.

The benefits to the review/appraisal process for probationary employees are shown in Figure 10.3.

Figure 10.3 Benefits of probation reviews

It is very important that all meetings which take place during the probationary period are notated in order to ensure a robust developmental progression for the employee during the period. The first meeting is likely to be a short introductory one, but the following meetings should give honest feedback on performance, anything that needs improving on, the timeline to make the improvement and details of any training that will be provided to help the employee improve their performance. Tact and diplomacy should inform all such review/appraisal meetings as staff will be anxious to attain permanency. It should also be remembered that the probationer is also deciding whether they think the setting is right for them.

A sample probation review/appraisal for an 6-month probation timetable might look as follows:

Name of Probationer: _____ Start Date: _____

Name of Supervisor: _____

Period of Probation: _____ Date of Determination: _____

Date of meeting	Issues arising	Actions agreed and training if required	Initials of both parties
Month 1			
Month 2			
Month __			
Month __			
Month __ – Final review/ appraisal			

At the end of the probation period there should be a final formal review/appraisal meeting which outlines whether the staff member will be kept on permanently and if any supports are felt necessary as they develop or settle into the role.

Openness, support and developmental encouragement should be the cornerstones of the probationary process. Approaching probationers' individual reviews/appraisals in an open, transparent and enabling procedure ensures that everybody wins.

Performance management and development

Organisations expect levels of performance from their staff in line with their contractual obligations and the needs of the organisation. People working together and co-operating with each other in organisations helps the work run smoothly. In ELC settings it is important that staff are aware that they work in settings where the best interests of the child are paramount. Human nature is such that we all differ in our approaches to the work we do, and some people are less conscientious than others. A performance management system offers opportunities and space to discuss the performance of all staff on an individual basis and at regular intervals.

Performance reviews can be a positive focus and they offer an opportunity to give staff feedback. A discussion about their performance will cover its impact, what works well, what needs improvement and how that improvement can be achieved. Pay increments and rewards may be made conditional on a satisfactory performance review or the achievement of improvements on an earlier review.

Some performance management systems use a rating for the performance of staff which is based on agreed criteria, feedback and analysis within the management team of the setting. Others are purely based on oversight of the challenges presented by the job and how people are managing any changes that might be implemented. Organisations differ in how they approach the concept and most adopt a best-fit model for appraisal/reviews. As a supervisor your approach should be developmental for the staff, informed by observation and by knowledge of changes that are taking place in ECL and the statutory responsibility you have for those you supervise.

Reviews are a two-way process and involve a considered approach to ensuring that staff feel supported, listened to and valued by the setting and are working well especially with the children in the setting.

Inspectors will examine the review processes to ensure that there is a robust process in place which will inform staff support and development. Reviews should be regular and focused feedback opportunities, not something to be feared, although there will be nervousness as a staff member awaits feedback. Realistically the outcome of a review should not be a surprise for any staff member as constant oversight, working partnership approaches and team structures within the ELC setting should ensure that a good working relationship already exists and is being reinforced by the formal review process. It should never be a box-ticking exercise – that would be to miss the opportunity to make your team a dynamic and holistic resource. Indeed the process should be strengthened by the experience of the staff member in supervision as they will be used to reflecting and considering how they can advance in their own practice, however it is very important that the two concepts, while they may complement each other, are not seen as one and the same.

Figure 10.4 Considerations for reviewers and reviewees

Performance review forms are an essential part of a robust review process and ensure that every employee is reviewed uniformly, in keeping with the principles of fairness and equality. Different formats may be developed for each level in the setting and each should be informed by the values, mission and goals of the setting.

THINK AND REFLECT

Below is a partial example of a review form for a care practitioner. Discuss the elements in the sample, ask to see one from your placement/practicum setting and draw up one you feel would be appropriate for any setting. Remember, the form must be signed by both reviewer and reviewee and should include a plan for development and training which might be identified in the process, so don't forget to include that on the form you design.

Practitioner

Name: _____

Position: _____

Supervisor/manager

Name: _____

Review date: _____

Current team responsibilities:

_____

_____

_____

Please rate your assessment (from 1 to 5, with 5 being the highest rating) of performance on the following:

1. Teamwork

Reviewee:

Rating: 1 → 2 → 3 → 4 → 5

Give two examples of how you feel you have reached that rating

_____

_____

Reviewer:

Rating: 1 → 2 → 3 → 4 → 5

Comments and observations

_____

_____

2. Supporting children in reaching their goals:

Reviewee:

Rating: 1 → 2 → 3 → 4 → 5

Give two examples of how you feel you have reached that rating

_____

_____

Reviewer:

Rating: 1 → 2 → 3 → 4 → 5

Comments and observations

_____

_____

CASE STUDY

Walter is due to have his first three-month review in his new job and is anxious that it goes well. He is worried about the fact that he is the first male employee ever to work in this specific ELC setting and that some parents have looked at him with suspicion in the room he works in. He is particularly worried that Mary's mother was very reluctant to allow him to work with Mary and has been offhand with him. Mary is a child with additional needs. Walter has endeavoured to support her development, and in fact his specialism is in additional needs. He has tried a number of interventions that have proved successful in supporting Mary's needs.

* How should Walter prepare for his review?
* What might be done to support Walter?
* What might be done to support Mary?

Continuing professional development (CPD)

Barnados describe continuing professional development (CPD) as 'any learning activities that you engage in consciously and proactively as a professional to develop and enhance your knowledge and skills' (Barnardos 2021, p. 3).

Embedded in *Nurturing Skills: The Workforce Plan for Early Learning and Care and School-Age Childcare, 2022–2028* (Government of Ireland 2022) is a recognition of the importance of CPD in supporting the developments that are envisaged in the ELC and SAC sector.

CPD for early years educators, SAC practitioners and childminders who are already qualified and working in the sector is a key factor in ensuring the quality of ELC and SAC provision. The literature review underpinning the OECD international project 'Quality beyond Regulation' concluded that: 'Participation in in-service training (or professional development) is the most consistent predictor of quality staff–child interactions, and also has direct links to child development and learning' (OECD 2018, p. 79).

Under Pillar 3 of the new Workforce Plan, CPD consists of:

* **Formal CPD:** intentional and structured and leading to formal qualification recognition and certification

* **Non-formal CPD:** intentional activities without certification, e.g. courses, webinars, communities of practice

* **Informal CPD:** enhancing everyday activities that will grow the experience of the learner such as including them in team meetings, online activities and professional networks.

There is a clear acknowledgement in the plan that the concept of CPD is not just a setting responsibility but is a shared responsibility between:

Figure 10.5 Shared responsibility for CPD (Workforce Plan, Pillar 3)

The problem identified in the Workforce Plan is that there is no uniformity of approach to CPD. The Child Care Act 1991 (Early Years Services) Regulations 2016 requires settings to have a staff training policy but it does not specify precisely what that training policy should look like. It requires the setting itself to set out how it identifies and addresses the training needs of employees and unpaid workers in the setting.

CPD is widely availed of by settings as a way to enhance the skills and internal progression plans for their staff, and in conjunction with the training fund it has enabled many practitioners to progress in their career paths. However, there are many operators in the area of CPD and there are opportunities to streamline the processes.

Pillar 3 of the Workforce Plan outlined above envisages:

* Developing a single national 'gateway' to access quality-assured CPD resources (both online and face-to-face, including resources to support informal types of CPD), with an online portal, and a national, online Learner Management System accessible to all ELC and SAC services and to all Early Years Educators, SAC practitioners, and childminders.

* Developing a national IT system to enable ELC and SAC services, Early Years Educators, SAC practitioners, and childminders, to record and monitor their participation in CPD activities – formal, non-formal and informal.

* The review of Síolta and the development of a single, national self-evaluation framework (both of which are commitments in First 5), building on the self-assessment tools already developed through the Aistear/Síolta Practice Guide and other resources. The development of a suite of resources and training programmes will support service providers and individuals to engage in reflective practice and to evaluate their own CPD needs.

* Strengthening quality assurance mechanisms for CPD opportunities and resources. While quality assurance of the content of CPD will continue to rely upon a range of structures already in place (e.g. the National Standards Authority of Ireland (NSAI) is currently responsible for quality assurance of CPD related to Síolta and Aistear, while the AIM working groups oversee training related to inclusion), a national mechanism will be established to provide oversight and governance of quality-assurance processes for CPD for the ELC and SAC workforce and to ensure that all CPD resources accessible through the national CPD 'gateway' are quality assured.

* Over time, this national structure of CPD for ELC and SAC will develop links with the national structure of CPD of primary school teachers. In line with First 5, opportunities for joint delivery of CPD programmes where appropriate will be considered.

Government of Ireland 2022

Records (both physical and online) of every worker's engagement with CPD, formal, non-formal and informal, will become a national priority. Structures and processes for quality assurance will be rolled out, funding will be introduced from September 2022 to support non-contact hours participation in CPD activities and guidance will be developed. This is a changing environment where CPD will not only be funded but will be required under the redeveloped approach which will amalgamate the frameworks such as Aistear, the Diversity, Equality and Inclusion Charter and Guidelines and the National Guidelines for SAC Services, which will ensure a cohesive, uniformly recognised suite of resources and training programmes to allow participation and individual recording and evaluation of the workers' CPD needs, which will feed into the review processes and will be enhanced in ELC and SAC developments.

CURRENT CPD RECORDS

As already mentioned, Regulation 9 of the Child Care Act 1991 (Early Years Services) Regulations 2016 requires that every setting has a staff training policy that sets out how the setting will support the training needs of their staff. However, CPD is also an individual responsibility that requires staff themselves to recognise what they need to develop as part of their own professional development journey and career path. The review process should support the individual staff member to acknowledge their current skill and competency level, determine what they might need to develop, and recognise opportunities to achieve that.

Staff should keep themselves informed about developments and opportunities to learn more and align their career plan to ensure they are focused, motivated, developing and continually learning. This can be done by developing a CPD plan and record system and an evaluation template which you can update as you progress through your plan.

An example of a CPD plan you could develop for your own purposes might look like this:

Name: _____

Current position: _____

Date and time of CPD undertaken	Learning undertaken	CPD credits if any	Learning outcome – how did it help your skills or competencies?	How it can be incorporated into your practice

Review and planning:

What I would like to learn/achieve now	How I plan to go about it

Signature:

Certificates to validate the CPD undertaken, copies of articles written, research read, peer reflection activities undertaken as listed above are attached as supporting documents

Certificate 1

Conference advertisement

etc.

Recap

1. **What is the difference between induction and probation? What different approaches would a supervisor take to each process?**

2. **What is CPD?**

3. **Name three types of CPD.**

References and further reading

Barnardos (2021) *Continuing Professional Development in Early Learning and Care*, Dublin: Barnardos and National Childhood Network

Government of Ireland (2022) *Nurturing Skills: The Workforce Plan for Early Learning and Care and School-Age Childcare, 2022–2028*. Dublin: Stationery Office <https://www.gov.ie/en/publication/97056-nurturing-skills-the-workforce-plan-for-early-learning-and-care-elc-and-school-age-childcare-sac-2022-2028>

OECD (2018) *Engaging with Young Children: Lessons from Research about Quality in Early Childhood Education and Care*. OECD

11

Employment Legislation

Learning Goals

In this chapter, learners will:

* Examine a selection of legislative requirements related to employees
* Learn about the national minimum wage

Introduction

Once you have selected the successful candidate and completed the steps described in Chapter 10, the person selected becomes an employee of the ECL setting. From that point, the employee is protected by employment legislation. Several pieces of legislation provide protections for the employee and the setting must comply with them.

While the first concern should be on developing a robust contract for all staff it is advisable that you consult a legal professional to draw up that contract; the detail is very important for the setting and its responsibilities, and for the employee and their rights and responsibilities.

The following is a brief snapshot of legislation which impacts on employers and their duties to employees. Employers should keep up to date with all legislation that relates to their responsibilities to their employees. They should understand that the contract between staff and employers is a two-way street which, if navigated correctly, ensures the journey is clear and unhindered.

Terms of Employment (Information) Act 1994 and 2014

This Act is one in a group of related Acts which include (as outlined by the Law Reform Commission):

* Terms of Employment (Information) Act 1994

* Protection of Employees (Part-Time Work) Act 2001 (as it relates to the 1994 Act)

* Industrial Relations (Amendment) Act 2012

* Local Government Reform Act 2014

The Act is particularly significant for new employees as it relates to the legal entitlement of every employee to receive a written copy of their employment contact and outlines what must be included in that contract.

Under Section 3 of the Act:

> **"** An employer must within 2 months after the commencement of an employee's employment with the employer, give or cause to be given to the employee a statement in writing containing the following particulars of the terms of the employee's employment, that is to say—
>
> (a) the full names of the employer and the employee,
>
> (b) the address of the employer in the State or, where appropriate, the address of the principal place of the relevant business of the employer in the State or the registered office (under Company Law) of the employer,
>
> (c) the place of work or, where there is no fixed or main place of work, a statement specifying that the employee is required or permitted to work at various places,
>
> (d) the title of the job or nature of the work for which the employee is employed,
>
> (e) the date of commencement of the employee's contract of employment,
>
> (f) in the case of a temporary contract of employment, the expected duration thereof or, if the contract of employment is for a fixed term, the date on which the contract expires, a reference to any registered employment agreement or employment regulation order which applies to the employee and confirmation of where the employee may obtain a copy of such agreement or order,

(g) the rate or method of calculation of the employee's remuneration and the pay reference period for the purposes of the National Minimum Wage Act 2000. The employee may, under section 23 of the National Minimum Wage Act 2000, request from the employer a written statement of the employee's average hourly rate of pay for any pay reference period as provided in that section,

(h) the length of the intervals between the times at which remuneration is paid, whether a week, a month or any other interval,

(i) any terms or conditions relating to hours of work (including overtime),

(j) any terms or conditions relating to paid leave (other than paid sick leave),

(k) any terms or conditions relating to—

(i) incapacity for work due to sickness or injury and paid sick leave, and

(ii) pensions and pension schemes,

(l) the period of notice which the employee is required to give and entitled to receive (whether by or under statute or under the terms of the employee's contract of employment) to determine the employee's contract of employment or, where this cannot be indicated when the information is given, the method for determining such periods of notice,

(m) a reference to any collective agreements which directly affect the terms and conditions of the employee's employment including, where the employer is not a party to such agreements, particulars of the bodies or institutions by whom they were made. **"**

Additional points to note under the Act include as follows:

✳ Such a contract statement is to be given to an employee even if the employee's employment ends before the end of the period within which the statement is required to be given (two months).

✳ A statement of contract furnished by an employer must be signed and dated by or on behalf of the employer.

✳ A copy of the contract must be retained by the employer during the period of the employee's employment and for a period of one year after.

✳ Where a contract has not been supplied to an existing employee (e.g. somebody who is in your employment since before the 1994 Act was passed) they can request a written contract and you must supply it within two months of the date the request is made.

✳ Where changes are made to the contract of employment (other than statutorily required changes) the employer shall notify the employee in writing of the nature and date of the change as soon after it happens but not later than one month after the change takes effect or, if an employee is required to work outside the state for more than one month, it should be given at the time of the employee's departure.

* Where an employer issues to an employee a contract of employment containing the particulars outlined, he or she must keep a copy of the statement for two years from the date on which that statement was issued and shall give that copy on demand to a social welfare inspector for inspection if requested.

* Failure to comply with this Act may be referred to the Workplace Relations Commission under the Workplace Relations Act 2015.

Providing a contract of employment ensures that there is transparency and fairness in the intentions of the employer, and while errors or omissions may arise and may be referred under the Workplace Relations Act 2015, for the most part the existence of and adherence to the terms of a contract of employment work for both employer and employee and ensure that people understand what is required of them in the workplace and what an employer can reasonably expect of them.

Employment Equality Acts 1998–2021

These Acts are among several related Acts (as outlined by the Law Reform Commission):

* Employment Equality Act 1998

* Equality Act 2004

* Protection of Employment (Exceptional Collective Redundancies and Related Matters) Act 2007

* Civil Law (Miscellaneous Provisions) Act 2008 (Part 16)

* Civil Law (Miscellaneous Provisions) Act 2011 (Sections 18–26)

* Equality (Miscellaneous Provisions) Act 2015 (Sections 3–11)

* Gender Pay Gap Information Act 2021 (Sections 2–4)

We have already outlined that the Acts must be taken into account in the selection process for every employee but it is significant for the working relationships of every employee in a setting and its operation comes under the auspices of the Minister for Children, Equality, Disability, Integration and Youth.

The Acts make it illegal to discriminate against an employee or prospective employee (including agency work providers and agency workers) on the basis of nine specific grounds in relation to: access to employment; conditions of employment; training or experience for or in relation to employment; promotion or re-grading; and classification of posts.

The nine grounds are outlined in Section 6 of the 1998 Act, amended by the Equality Act 2004:

> **"** (1) [D]iscrimination shall be taken to occur when:
>
> (a) a person is treated less favourably than another person is, has been or would be treated in a comparable situation on any of the grounds specified in subsection (2) (in this Act referred to as the 'discriminatory grounds') which—
>
> (i) exists,
>
> (ii) existed but no longer exists,
>
> (iii) may exist in the future, or
>
> (iv) is imputed to the person concerned,
>
> (b) a person who is associated with another person—
>
> (i) is treated, by virtue of that association, less favourably than a person who is not so associated is, has been or would be treated in a comparable situation, and
>
> (ii) similar treatment of that other person on any of the discriminatory grounds would, by virtue of paragraph (a), constitute discrimination.
>
> (2) As between any two persons, the discriminatory grounds (and the descriptions of those grounds for the purposes of this Act) are—
>
> (a) that one is a woman and the other is a man (in this Act referred to as 'the gender ground'),
>
> (b) that they are of different civil status (in this Act referred to as 'the civil status ground'),
>
> (c) that one has family status and the other does not (in this Act referred to as 'the family status ground'),
>
> (d) that they are of different sexual orientation (in this Act referred to as 'the sexual orientation ground'),
>
> (e) that one has a different religious belief from the other, or that one has a religious belief and the other has not (in this Act referred to as 'the religion ground'),
>
> (f) that they are of different ages, but subject to subsection (3) (in this Act referred to as 'the age ground'),

(g) that one is a person with a disability and the other either is not or is a person with a different disability (in this Act referred to as 'the disability ground'),

(h) that they are of different race, colour, nationality or ethnic or national origins (in this Act referred to as 'the ground of race'),

(i) that one is a member of the Traveller community and the other is not (in this Act referred to as 'the Traveller community ground'). **"**

For the purposes of the Act:

"'Traveller community' means the community of people commonly so called who are identified (both by themselves and others) as people with a shared history, culture and traditions including, historically, a nomadic way of life on the island of Ireland.

Discrimination on the 'gender ground' shall be taken to occur where, on a ground related to her pregnancy or maternity leave, a woman employee is treated, contrary to any statutory requirement, less favourably than another employee is, has been or would be treated.

The 'age ground' applies only in relation to persons above the maximum age at which a person is statutorily obliged to attend school and an employer may set a minimum age, not exceeding 18 years, for recruitment to a post. **"**

Section 8(6) of the Act provides that:

"an employer shall be taken to discriminate against an employee or prospective employee in relation to conditions of employment if, on any of the discriminatory grounds, the employer does not offer or afford to that employee or prospective employee or to a class of persons of whom he or she is one—

(a) the same terms of employment (other than remuneration and pension rights),

(b) the same working conditions, and

(c) the same treatment in relation to overtime, shift work, short time, transfers, lay-offs, redundancies, dismissals and disciplinary measures, as the employer offers or affords to another person or class of persons, where the circumstances in which both such persons or classes are or would be employed are not materially different. **"**

For those who do engage employees and for the employees themselves it is very important to comply with the specifics of the Acts to ensure that people know that they have been fairly and equally treated.

The Gender Pay Gap Information Act 2021 adds a certain accountability to the equality required in the recruitment process and requires:

"(a) employers to publish information relating to the remuneration of their employees for the purpose of showing whether there are differences in such remuneration referable to gender and, if so, the size of such differences,

(b) that information referred to in paragraph (a) include the following:

(i) the difference between the mean hourly remuneration of employees of the male gender and that of employees of the female gender expressed as a percentage;

(ii) the difference between the median hourly remuneration of employees of the male gender and that of employees of the female gender expressed as a percentage;

(iii) the difference between the mean bonus remuneration of employees of the male gender and that of employees of the female gender expressed as a percentage;

(iv) the difference between the median bonus remuneration of employees of the male gender and that of employees of the female gender expressed as a percentage;

(v) the difference between the mean hourly remuneration of part-time employees of the male gender and that of part-time employees of the female gender expressed as a percentage;

(vi) the difference between the median hourly remuneration of part-time employees of the male gender and that of part-time employees of the female gender expressed as a percentage;

(vii) the percentage of all employees of the male gender who were paid bonus remuneration and the percentage of all employees of the female gender who were paid such remuneration;

(viii) the percentage of all employees of the male gender who received benefits in kind and the percentage of all employees of the female gender who received such benefits, "

and:

> (c) employers [are] to publish, concurrently with the publication of information referred to in this section that shows differences relating to remuneration that are referable to gender, a statement setting out—
>
> (i) in the employer's opinion, the reasons for such differences in that employer's case, and
>
> (ii) the measures (if any) being taken, or proposed to be taken, by the employer to eliminate or reduce such differences in that employer's case.

The effect of this addition is that not only do employers have to explain what differences there are, how they are being justified and how many people are affected by the differences, but also what they are going to do about them.

Finally, the Gender Pay Gap Information Act 2021 also protects an employee from victimisation (dismissal or other unfavourable treatment) as a reaction to:

> (a) a complaint of discrimination made by the employee to the employer,
>
> (b) any proceedings by a complainant,
>
> (c) an employee having represented or otherwise supported a complainant,
>
> (d) the work of an employee having been compared with that of another employee for any of the purposes of this Act or any enactment repealed by this Act,
>
> (e) an employee having been a witness in any proceedings under this Act or the Equal Status Act 2000 or any such repealed enactment,
>
> (f) an employee having opposed by lawful means an act which is unlawful under this Act or the said Act of 2000 or which was unlawful under any such repealed enactment, or
>
> (g) an employee having given notice of an intention to take any of the actions mentioned in the preceding paragraphs.
>
> As evident from the Employment Equality Acts 1998–2021, compliance is required even before a person is a fully contracted employee and it is therefore an integral part of the recruitment process as it informs the process of advertisement, shortlisting and selection of employees.

Equal Status Acts 2000–2018

This is another group of Acts:

* Equal Status Act 2000

* Intoxicating Liquor Act 2003 (Section 25)

* Equality Act 2004 (Part 3)

* Civil Law (Miscellaneous Provisions) Act 2008 (Part 14)

* Civil Law (Miscellaneous Provisions) Act 2011 (Section 21, referring to Section 21 of the Equal Status Act 2000)

* Equal Status (Amendment) Act 2012

* Equality (Miscellaneous Provisions) Act 2015 (Sections 12–15)

The Act (which even though it includes other Acts, is still referred to as an Act because technically it is a consolidated Act) relies on the nine grounds of discrimination which are outlined above in the Employment Equality Acts 1998-2021 (pp. 141–2):

* Membership of the Traveller community

* Race

* Religion

* Age

* Marital Status

* Sexuality

* Gender

* Family Status

* Disability

The 2000 Act specifically relates to the provision of goods, services, accommodation and education and the treatment of people who access those services, including rent supplement, housing assistance or social welfare payments. The Act also provides for investigation and remedying of certain types of discrimination, whether direct or indirect. Additionally it provides for powers of inspection to the Workplace Relations Commission (which may award redress) in relation to possible breaches under Section 27 of the Workplace Relations Act 2015.

In relation to recruitment, it is important to be aware of this Act and to ensure that you provide reasonable accommodation for people with disabilities or additional learning needs whom you may recruit.

Section 2 specifies that 'disability' means:

> **"**(a) the total or partial absence of a person's bodily or mental functions, including the absence of a part of a person's body,
>
> (b) the presence in the body of organisms causing, or likely to cause, chronic disease or illness,
>
> (c) the malfunction, malformation or disfigurement of a part of a person's body,
>
> (d) a condition or malfunction which results in a person learning differently from a person without the condition or malfunction, or
>
> (e) a condition, disease or illness which affects a person's thought processes, perception of reality, emotions or judgement or which results in disturbed behaviour. **"**

Remembering that the Act relates to actual and potential employees would indicate that if informed of a person's additional need then the employer should carry out a needs assessment to ensure that the person is provided the reasonable accommodation that is required under the Act.

The Act is specific about what would constitute discrimination in the case of people with a disability. Section 4 provides:

(1) For the purposes of this Act discrimination includes a refusal or failure by the provider of a service to do all that is reasonable to accommodate the needs of a person with a disability by providing special treatment or facilities, if without such special treatment or facilities it would be impossible or unduly difficult for the person to avail himself or herself of the service.

(2) A refusal or failure to provide the special treatment or facilities to which subsection (1) refers shall not be deemed reasonable unless such provision would give rise to a cost, other than a nominal cost, to the provider of the service in question.

(3) A refusal or failure to provide the special treatment or facilities to which subsection (1) refers does not constitute discrimination if, by virtue of another provision of this Act, a refusal or failure to provide the service in question to that person would not constitute discrimination.

(4) Where a person has a disability that, in the circumstances, could cause harm to the person or to others, treating the person differently to the extent reasonably necessary to prevent such harm does not constitute discrimination.

(5) This section is without prejudice to the provisions of sections 7(2)(a), 9(a) and 15(2)(g) of the Education Act, 1998, in so far as they relate to functions of the Minister for Education and Science, recognised schools and boards of management in regard to students with a disability.

Section 5 of the Act provides some exceptions for what might be considered reasonable grounds to differentiate such as pensions, insurance and other specifically explained reasons. In general, however, the Act is written to ensure that such instances are the exception and not the rule.

Extend Your Learning

Watch the video on the Equal Status Acts at www.ihrec.ie/guides-and-tools/human-rights-and-equality-in-the-provision-of-good-and-services/what-does-the-law-say/equal-status-acts/

Read Section 5 of the Equal Status Acts 2000–2018 and examine the exemptions listed in that section. Do you think all those exemptions are reasonable? Are there any others you think should be added?

With the requirement for ELCs to introduce and use the concept of universal design in the care and learning of all children it would be reasonable to expect that ELC settings would be at the forefront of providing the additional supports that are envisaged in this Act and plan for the needs or new recruits and the universal acceptance of all people in the setting. Universal design (UD) is the design and composition of an environment so it can be accessed, understood and used to the greatest extent possible by all people, regardless of their age, size, ability or disability (Government of Ireland, 2019 p. 4).

Safety, Health and Welfare at Work Act 2005

Other relevant Acts in this area include:

* Chemicals Act 2008 (Section 37)

* Chemicals (Amendment) Act 2010 (Section 1)

* Industrial Development (Forfás Dissolution) Act 2014 (Part 7)

The Act specifies general duties of employers in Section 8:

> (1) Every employer shall ensure, so far as is reasonably practicable, the safety, health and welfare at work of his or her employees.
>
> (2) Without prejudice to the generality of subsection (1), the employer's duty extends, in particular, to the following:
>
> (a) managing and conducting work activities in such a way as to ensure, so far as is reasonably practicable, the safety, health and welfare at work of his or her employees;
>
> (b) managing and conducting work activities in such a way as to prevent, so far as is reasonably practicable, any improper conduct or behaviour likely to put the safety, health or welfare at work of his or her employees at risk;
>
> (c) as regards the place of work concerned, ensuring, so far as is reasonably practicable—
>
>   (i) the design, provision and maintenance of it in a condition that is safe and without risk to health,
>
>   (ii) the design, provision and maintenance of safe means of access to and egress from it, and

(iii) the design, provision and maintenance of plant and machinery or any other articles that are safe and without risk to health;

(d) ensuring, so far as it is reasonably practicable, the safety and the prevention of risk to health at work of his or her employees relating to the use of any article or substance or the exposure to noise, vibration or ionising or other radiations or any other physical agent;

(e) providing systems of work that are planned, organised, performed, maintained and revised as appropriate so as to be, so far as is reasonably practicable, safe and without risk to health;

(f) providing and maintaining facilities and arrangements for the welfare of his or her employees at work;

(g) providing the information, instruction, training and supervision necessary to ensure, so far as is reasonably practicable, the safety, health, and welfare at work of his or her employees;

(h) determining and implementing the safety, health and welfare measures necessary for the protection of the safety, health and welfare of his or her employees when identifying hazards and carrying out a risk assessment under section 19 or when preparing a safety statement under section 20 and ensuring that the measures take account of changing circumstances and the general principles of prevention specified in Schedule 3;

(i) having regard to the general principles of prevention in Schedule 3, where risks cannot be eliminated or adequately controlled or in such circumstances as may be prescribed, providing and maintaining such suitable protective clothing and equipment as is necessary to ensure, so far as is reasonably practicable, the safety, health and welfare at work of his or her employees;

(j) preparing and revising, as appropriate, adequate plans and procedures to be followed and measures to be taken in the case of an emergency or serious and imminent danger;

(k) reporting accidents and dangerous occurrences, as may be prescribed, to the Authority or to a person prescribed under section 33, as appropriate, and

(l) obtaining, where necessary, the services of a competent person (whether under a contract of employment or otherwise) for the purpose of ensuring, so far as is reasonably practicable, the safety, health and welfare at work of his or her employees. 〞

The responsibilities of the employer are far-ranging and include identifying potential hazards, preparing a safety statement, ongoing maintenance of equipment, reporting accidents and providing instruction, training and supervision.

Under Section 10(3) of the Act, training should be provided:

> "(a) on recruitment,
>
> (b) in the event of the transfer of an employee or change of task assigned to an employee,
>
> (c) on the introduction of new work equipment, systems of work or changes in existing work equipment or systems of work, and
>
> (d) on the introduction of new technology "

The responsibility goes both ways. In Section 13, the Act sets out the duties of the employee:

> "(a) comply with the relevant statutory provisions, as appropriate, and take reasonable care to protect his or her safety, health and welfare and the safety, health and welfare of any other person who may be affected by the employee's acts or omissions at work,
>
> (b) ensure that he or she is not under the influence of an intoxicant to the extent that he or she is in such a state as to endanger his or her own safety, health or welfare at work or that of any other person,
>
> (c) if reasonably required by his or her employer, submit to any appropriate, reasonable and proportionate tests for intoxicants by, or under the supervision of, a registered medical practitioner who is a competent person, as may be prescribed,
>
> (d) co-operate with his or her employer or any other person so far as is necessary to enable his or her employer or the other person to comply with the relevant statutory provisions, as appropriate,
>
> (e) not engage in improper conduct or other behaviour that is likely to endanger his or her own safety, health and welfare at work or that of any other person,
>
> (f) attend such training and, as appropriate, undergo such assessment as may reasonably be required by his or her employer or as may be prescribed relating to safety, health and welfare at work or relating to the work carried out by the employee,

(g) having regard to his or her training and the instructions given by his or her employer, make correct use of any article or substance provided for use by the employee at work or for the protection of his or her safety, health and welfare at work, including protective clothing or equipment,

(h) report to his or her employer or to any other appropriate person, as soon as practicable—

(i) any work being carried on, or likely to be carried on, in a manner which may endanger the safety, health or welfare at work of the employee or that of any other person,

(ii) any defect in the place of work, the systems of work, any article or substance which might endanger the safety, health or welfare at work of the employee or that of any other person, or

(iii) any contravention of the relevant statutory provisions which may endanger the safety, health and welfare at work of the employee or that of any other person,

of which he or she is aware.

(2) An employee shall not, on entering into a contract of employment, misrepresent himself or herself to an employer with regard to the level of training as may be prescribed under subsection (1)(f). **"**

This final part is the reason why all qualifications, training and other material provided by a new employee must be checked at the start of their employment – for their own safety and the safety of all others in the ELC setting, especially the children. Every stakeholder has a part to play in making the setting a safe one for everyone.

The National Vetting Bureau (Children and Vulnerable Persons) Act 2012

This Act, focused on the protection of children and vulnerable people, supports the establishment and maintenance of a national vetting bureau database. Vetting must take place before any person is employed in any capacity within ELC settings and from April 2016 it is a criminal offence to employ anybody who has not complied with this Act. Therefore everyone working in an ELC setting must have completed the Garda vetting process.

ELC services must now have a Garda National Vetting Bureau (GNVB) affiliate registration number as it facilitates traceability since the number remains with the person vetted.

Other employment legislation

There are many other pieces of legislation whose implications can impact on the day-to-day running of an ELC setting from time to time, depending on the specific circumstances of each employee or team member and the modes of operation of staff teams and shifts as they may arise. A synopsis of various pieces of legislation is included here for information purposes only and should not form any legal definition.

The focus of a contract may be geared to the requirements of the main employment legislation above and satisfying the detail within those pieces of legislation, but the following legislation also needs to be incorporated into any contract for staff. This can be done by noting that the contract 'takes account of ...' or 'is also subject to ...', for instance.

ORGANISATION OF WORKING TIME ACT 1997

Breaks and rest periods

This Act specifies that employees should have adequate breaks during their working day and specifically that they should be given:

Daily:

* A rest period of not less than 11 consecutive hours in each 24-hour period he/she works for his/her employer

* A break of at least 15 minutes in a 4.5 hour period of work

* A 30-minute break in a six-hour work period (the 30 minutes can include the 15 minutes above)

* The Minister can under regulations allow for more than the 30 minutes above but not more than one hour.

* A break at the end of the day does not satisfy either the 15 minutes or the 30 minutes above.

Weekly:

* A rest period of at least 24 consecutive hours

* If the 24 consecutive hours rest in the seven-day period is not possible there should be two rest periods of 24 consecutive hours in the following seven-day period.

Reference period:

* Employees should not work in excess of an average of 48 hours per week for what is called a reference period, which is calculated over four months of consecutive days.

Working time information

* If start and finish times are not included in the contract of employment, the employee must be given at least 24 hours' notice before they are due to start.

* If additional hours are required to be worked there should also be 24 hours' notice.

Annual leave

* Four working weeks in a leave year when the employee works at least 1,365 hours (unless in a year they change employment)

* One-third of a working week for every month in a leave year where the employee has worked at least 117 hours

    or:

* Eight per cent of the hours the employee works in a leave year (but only to a maximum of four working weeks)

* Work requirements may determine the time at which the annual leave is granted as long as the employer takes into account the needs of the employee to facilitate family responsibilities and to give an opportunity to the employee to avail of rest and recreation

* With agreement the annual leave can be taken within a period of six months after the leave year (carried over with agreement)

* If the employee has been sick and has provided a medical certificate to that effect then the carry over period can extend to 15 months.

* Pay should be in advance of taking the leave.

Public holidays

Provided that the employee has worked at least 40 hours in the five weeks ending on the day of the public holiday they should have:

* A paid day off on that day

* Or a paid day off within a month of that day

* Or an additional day of annual leave

* Or an additional day's pay.

Records

* Records of time off and annual leave must be kept available for inspection and must be kept for three years.

EMPLOYMENT (MISCELLANEOUS PROVISIONS) ACT 2018

This Act provides that within five days of starting employment the employers must give an employee notice in writing of:

1. The full names of the employer and the employee;

2. The address of the employer;

3. The expected duration of the contract, in the case of a temporary contract, or the end date if the contract is a fixed-term contract;

4. The rate or method of calculation of the employee's pay;

5. The number of hours the employer reasonably expects the employee to work per normal working day and per normal working week.

This is referred to as a 'Day 5 Statement' and is in addition to the requirement to give a written contract within two months of commencing employment.

NATIONAL MINIMUM WAGE ACT 2009 (UPDATED 2022)

This sets out the minimum hourly wages an employee should receive (effective from 1 January 2022):

Age	Amount	% of NMW
Under 18	€7.35	70%
18	€8.40	80%
19	€9.45	90%
NMW rate	€10.50	100%

There is a proposal to introduce a national living wage, which is basically a minimum wage that takes inflation into account, so that everyone in the country, whatever their circumstances, would have a minimum level of income. In Ireland, during the Covid-19 pandemic, we had a hint of how this might work in the form of the PUP payment. People received a certain amount of money to ensure that they had enough to cover their living needs. Currently there are different payments for people on different social welfare payments, which creates a complicated system, and it is felt that a national living wage would make the system easier to administer.

CARER'S LEAVE ACT 2001

This relates to the entitlement of an employee to unpaid leave from their employment to allow them to personally provide full-time care and attention to a person who needs such care.

The Act allows for:

* Minimum of 13 weeks or maximum of 104 weeks for any one care recipient as long as:
  — there is at least 12 months' continuous service with the employer before the leave starts

* The intention is to give the care personally to the person needing the care (decided by Department of Employment Affairs and Social Protection officers duly appointed)

* Care is actually given for all of the leave given

* Written notice of the intention to take care leave must be given in writing at least six weeks before the leave is proposed to begin

* Refusal on reasonable written grounds may be given

* The employee can avail of education or training during the care leave as long as they do not exceed 18.5 hours per week of such training or education.

Parental Leave Acts 1998–2019

This set of Acts includes:

* Parental Leave Act 1998

* Parental Leave (Amendment) Act 2006

* Parental Leave (Amendment) Act 2019

The main provisions of the Act are:

* A parent must have worked for their employer for a full year before they apply for the leave

* Each parent is entitled to 26 working weeks' (six months') **unpaid** parental leave, which must be taken before the child is 12 years of age or, in the case of children with disabilities (or long-term illness), before the child is 16 years of age.

* There is limited paid leave (force majeure leave) to allow employees deal with family emergencies as a result of illness or injury of a family member (up to three days in 12 consecutive months or five days in 36 consecutive months).

* It includes both part-time employees and fixed-term employees (where length of contract is specific and terminates when the date is reached).

* It also allows that in the case of adoption the adoptive parent will be entitled to parental leave (originally two weeks but recently extended to five weeks by the Family Leave and Miscellaneous Provisions Act 2021).

* It cannot be transferred between parents unless both work for the same employer and it has been agreed with that employer and the maximum leave one parent in that situation can take is 14 weeks

* It can be taken as continuous weeks or in two periods of continuous tranches, each consisting of not less than six weeks, and there must be a gap of 10 weeks between each tranche.

* Notice in writing must be given at least six weeks before the leave commences with the detail of what is proposed to be taken.

* It should be signed off on by the employer four weeks before it is due to start.

Under Section 13, force majeure leave applies to:

> "(a) a person of whom the employee is the parent or adoptive parent,
>
> (b) the spouse of the employee or a person with whom the employee is living as husband or wife,
>
> (c) a person to whom the employee is *in loco parentis*,
>
> (d) a brother or sister of the employee,
>
> (e) a parent or grandparent of the employee,
> and
> a person other than one specified in any of paragraphs (a) to (e), who resides with the employee in a relationship of domestic dependency. "

Paternity Leave and Benefit Act 2016 (revised 2021)

This Act, while affirming the rights already set out in the Parental Leave Acts 1998–2019, provides for the protection of the parent's employment rights while on paternity leave.

Section 19 provides that protection as follows:

> "(1) During a period of absence from work by an employee while on paternity leave, the employee shall be deemed to have been in the employment of the employer and, accordingly, while so absent the employee shall, subject to subsection (4) and section 21, be treated as if she or he had not been so absent; and such absence shall not affect any right related to the employee's employment (other than the employee's right to remuneration during such absence), whether conferred by statute, contract or otherwise.
>
> (2) A period of absence from work whilst on paternity leave shall not be treated as part of any other leave (including sick leave, annual leave, additional maternity leave, subsection (1)(a) leave or subsection (1)(b) leave within the meaning of section 16 of the Act of 1994, adoptive leave or additional adoptive leave within the meaning of the Act of 1995) to which the employee concerned is entitled.

(3) Where an employee who is—

(a) on probation in his or her employment,

(b) undergoing training in relation to that employment, or (c) employed under a contract of apprenticeship,

takes paternity leave, and his or her employer considers that the employee's absence from his or her employment while on such leave would not be consistent with the continuance of the probation, training or apprenticeship, the employer may require that the probation, training or apprenticeship shall stand suspended during the period of leave concerned and be completed by the employee at the end of that period.

(4) An employee shall be deemed not to be an employed contributor for the purposes of the Act of 2005 for any contribution week within the meaning of that Act in a period of absence from work on paternity leave if the employee does not receive any reckonable earnings within the meaning of that Act in respect of that week. **"**

Section 20 provides that each of the following shall be void:

" (a) any purported termination of employment of an employee while the employee is absent from work on paternity leave;

(b) any purported suspension from employment of an employee while the employee is absent from work on paternity leave;

(c) any notice of termination of the employment of an employee given while the employee is absent from work on paternity leave. **"**

Where termination notice has been served immediately prior to the parent taking the leave, that termination is extended for the duration of the paternal leave.

The Act further provides for the conditions where the parent on paternity leave can claim and receive paternity benefit during that paternity leave period and details specifics around the amount that will be paid by the state.

The employee is entitled to return to the job they did prior to the paternity leave, at the rate that they would be entitled to even if they had not left including any increases that would have been applied while they were on leave and no changes should have been made to their contract of employment.

Adoptive Leave Acts 2005

This is an amalgamation of two Acts:

* Adoptive Leave Act 1995

* Adoptive Leave Act 2005

It is intended to provide protection against unfair dismissal where people take leave for the purposes of child adoption.

* An employed adopting mother (or sole male adopter) can take leave for a minimum period of 16 weeks (can be extended for a maximum of eight weeks).

* Where the adopting mother dies, the adopting father may be entitled to adoptive leave for the remainder of the 16 weeks from the date of her death, which could also be extended if agreed by eight weeks maximum.

* An employee (with some exceptions) is entitled to time off work without loss of pay to attend any pre-adoption classes and meetings that they are obliged to attend.

* It provides procedures to be followed with regard to notices to be given of leave, return to work and in relation to changes in ownership of the business while the person was on adoptive leave.

Maternity Protection Acts 1994 and 2004

This includes:

* Maternity Protection Act 1994

* Maternity Protection (Amendment) Act 2004

This Act is intended to provide protection to the safety and health at work of pregnant workers or those workers who have recently given birth or are breastfeeding and to entitle a male employee to leave in certain cases where the mother of his child dies and to extend protection against unfair dismissal.

Among other things the Act provides for the following:

* A pregnant employee is entitled to maternity leave for a minimum period of not less than 26 weeks (six months), which can be postponed if necessary or extended with consent.

* Such leave can start four weeks before the confinement or at least two weeks beforehand.

* There should be a minimum of four weeks' written notice to the employer that the leave will commence.

* A certificate of pregnancy and expected week of confinement should be given to the employer.

* Maternity leave can be extended.

* It can also be postponed in circumstances where the child is hospitalised, provided this is after four weeks from the date of confinement and can be reinstated not later than seven days after the discharge of the child from hospital.

* For ante-natal or post-natal care or both an employee is entitled to time off from work without loss of pay to attend one set of ante-natal classes (other than the last three classes) and the father (with some exceptions) is entitled to similarly attend the last two ante-natal classes attended by the expectant mother of their child.

* Breastfeeding employees are entitled to time off without loss of pay for breastfeeding in the workplace where facilities for breastfeeding are provided or a reduction in her working hours to breastfeed other than in her workplace.

* The Act also provides for similar provisions for fathers where the mother dies.

Protection of Employees (Fixed-Term Work) Act 2003

This Act provides that for the most part an employee who has a fixed end date for their employment cannot be treated differently from an employee who does not have a fixed-term contract.

Exceptions can be made for:

* Pensions, objective grounds (e.g. renewing a fixed-term contract with a further fixed-term contract as long as the decision is not based on the fact that the person is on a fixed-term contract – for example if the contract were for a fixed term to get a specific job done, the contract would be just until that job was done even if the term needed to be extended to get that specific job done) and there may be an allowance for pro-rata pension entitlements for the ratio of time that the contract covers compared to full time provision. Thus there is no incentive for a person to deliberately delay the work in order to better their pension entitlements because to do so would be unfair to the employer.

* Where an employee completes or has completed three years' continuous employment with his or her employer or associated employer (any or all of the three years' service may have occurred prior to the passing of the Act) the employer may renew the contract for a fixed term on one occasion only and that renewal may be for a period of no longer than one year.

Industrial Relations (Amendment) Act 2015

This Act is one of a group of Acts that includes:

* Unfair Dismissals Act 1977

* Worker Protection (Regular Part-Time Employees) Act 1991 insofar as it relates to the Unfair Dismissals Acts 1977 and 1991 (repealed)

* Unfair Dismissals (Amendment) Act 1993

* Protection of Employees (Part-Time Work) Act 2001 insofar as it relates to the Unfair Dismissals Acts 1977 to 1993

* Civil Service Regulation (Amendment) Act 2005 (Part 6)

* Protection of Employment (Exceptional Collective Redundancies and Related Matters) Act 2007

* Industrial Relations (Amendment) Act 2015 (Section 39)

The most important consideration here is that every dismissal is automatically deemed to be unfair and it is the responsibility of the employer to prove that it is fair.

The duty of care afforded all staff in an ELC setting requires that the fundamentals of employment legislation and its application to the staff in the setting is robustly understood and implemented throughout the recruitment, employment and development of staff within the setting.

Recap

1. **What is the national minimum wage (NMW)?**

2. **What is proposed to replace the NMW?**

3. **What break(s) should there be in a standard six-hour working day?**

4. **Name four pieces of legislation an employee should be familiar with.**

5. **What does GNVB stand for?**

6. **How soon after being appointed should an employee get a copy of their contract of employment?**

7. **What is a 'Day 5 Statement'?**

Inspection Processes

Learning Goals

In this chapter, learners will:

* Examine the legislation that covers the processes of inspection in ELC settings

* Learn how different inspection processes work

* Learn about compliance and non-compliance and the implications of non-compliance

Introduction

Regulations, legislation and statutory provisions have no effect unless there are robust measures, sanctions and supports to ensure compliance with them. This is never more significant than in ELC settings where children aged 0–6 years are cared for and have experiences that support their learning and development in safe, secure and compliant settings.

There is effectively a dual inspection process in the ELC sector currently: Tusla inspects compliance with regulations and law; and the DoE has the responsibility to evaluate the early educational experiences of children participating in the ECCE scheme.

Children's rights are fundamental considerations in any setting and the protections afforded children under our Constitution, the UN Convention on the Rights of the Child (UNCRC) and under our legislation underpin inspection of all ELC settings and in the process ensure that we can stand over the quality of the services offered within those settings and the protection of children who attend them.

Legislation relating to inspections

The inspection process undertaken by Tusla is intended to ensure compliance with the following legislation:

* Child Care Act 1991 (Early Years Services) Regulations 2016: the statutory instrument for the regulation of early years services catering for children under the age of 6 years who are not attending primary school.

* Child Care Act 1991 (Early Years Services) (Amendments) Regulations 2016, which made slight amendments to the 2016 regulations

* Part 12 of the Child and Family Agency Act amended the Child Care Act 1991 (as inserted in Section 92 of the Child and Family Agency Act 2013). This is known as Part VIIA, and describes the legal provisions for the supervision of early years services.

Tusla inspections

Tusla inspections are carried out by eight regional inspectorate teams and are co-ordinated and managed nationally. Data is reviewed nationally and regionally to ensure optimum use of resources so that services which present the highest risk are inspected more frequently (Tusla 2021).

The inspection process undertaken by Tusla is aimed at ensuring that:

* The service is well governed

* The health, welfare and development of each child is supported

* Children are safe in the service

* The premises are safe, suitable and appropriate for the care and education of children.

These considerations inform best practice in relation to the principles of inspection (Tusla 2021).

Evidence-based enforcement — Data and information support for inspections: which settings are reviewed and how frequently

Selectivity — Prioritisation is used to determine where to allocate resources

Risk focus and proportionality — The annual inspection programme is based on and aligned to the level of risk posed to children

Responsive regulation — Higher numbers of non-compliances or identified risks result in increased frequency of inspections

Long-term vision — The inspectorate operates within a three-year regulatory strategy

Co-ordination and consolidation — The inspectorate co-ordinates inspection activities with other inspectorates

Transparent governance — Inspection reports, enforcement activity and the inspectorate processes are published, and there is regular communication with the sector

Information integration — Websites, ezines, emails, letters and regulatory notices are used in order to share information

Clear and fair process — Right of reply to inspection findings for providers; inspection reports and processes are published

Compliance promotion — Compliance tools, industry guidance and self-assessment tools are made available online

Professionalism — Inspectors commit to continuous training aligned to the annual training plan

Figure 12.1 Tusla inspections

FREQUENCY OF INSPECTIONS

Inspections are carried out on an annual inspection programme basis. While inspections will be prioritised based on the level of risk and the efficient use of resources for the process, an inspection will take place at a minimum once in a registration (three-year) cycle. This is apart from the initial new service fit-for-purpose inspection, which examines the suitability of the premises. A fit-for-purpose inspection would also be carried out if there were a change of use, extension, or change of registration category.

Note: The majority of inspections are unannounced.

INSPECTION PROCEDURE

* The inspector carries out **preparatory work** to determine the type and scope of the inspection:

    — If it is a fit-for-purpose first inspection then the inspector will review all documentation provided for registration.

    — If it is an unannounced inspection of a previously inspected setting then the inspector will review previous inspection reports and any other information that is available (e.g. feedback and concerns forms [submitted to the Early Years Inspectorate], changes in circumstances, etc.).

* The inspector carries out an **on-site inspection**, which is unannounced in most circumstances. As an authorised person, the inspector holds a warrant to conduct inspections under Section 58I(1) of the Child Care Act 1991, which will be presented on arrival at the setting. The inspector will hold a preliminary meeting with the registered provider or designated person in charge on the day and verify registration details at that meeting. If there have been changes, the registered provider will have to submit a change in circumstances form to the Registration Office of the Early Years Inspectorate.

* The inspection will use the **triangulation method** to collate evidence, involving reviewing documentation (records, policies, procedures, rosters, etc.); observing practices in the setting (relationships, interactions and pedagogical practice); and interviews and consultation with management and staff.

* There will be a full **walk-through** of the premises to assess security, suitability and equipment while also observing other legislative requirements – the inspector can ascertain if any other legislative requirements are not being complied with and can inform other inspection processes associated with that legislation (e.g. fire safety, lighting, food safety and hygiene); details of this are included in Appendix 2 of the *Guide to Inspection in Early Years Services* (Tusla 2021).

* At the end of the inspection there will be a **conclusion meeting** with the registered provider or designated person in charge and any non-compliance issues will be discussed along with any breaches of regulations. Corrective actions and recommendations on practice will be shared. The inspector will give a clear indication of what the findings are and will give the provider or person in charge the right to reply, to amend or update the report. A timescale will be given for the issuing of the draft inspection report.

* The inspector will identify both **compliance** (being met) and **non-compliance** (not being met) in relation to regulations pertinent to the service being inspected. At the end of the process all non-compliances will be noted and recorded in the inspection report.

* Where there is non-compliance identified that is deemed to pose a **significant risk** to the safety, health and welfare of children, an Immediate Action Notice will be issued. This requires an immediate response which will outline what actions will be taken immediately to eliminate the risk that has been identified.

* An **initial report** is drafted by the inspection team. It contains details of the inspection, registration details, areas of compliance and areas of non-compliance, along with a list of the potential impact or risks posed by the non-compliance issues.

* A draft inspection report and **Factual Accuracy Form** is sent to the registered service provider. Doing this allows for a right of reply and an opportunity to correct any factual errors. The service provider is given a timescale to reply and then the submission will be reviewed before the inspection report is finalised.

* If a setting is **fully compliant** and the report has been reviewed and the Factual Accuracy Form returned, the report is finalised and published on the Early Years Inspectorate website.

* If a setting is **non-compliant**, a Factual Accuracy Form and a request for a **corrective and preventive action** (CAPA) plan for the non-compliances identified will be issued to the registered provider.

* After the **CAPA response** (see below), if the inspector is satisfied that the non-compliance has been rectified the report can be finalised and published on the Early Years Inspectorate website.

* If the non-compliances are not satisfied in the CAPA response, the registered provider may be requested to submit a second CAPA response or may be called to attend a **regulatory compliance meeting** with the inspector and the inspection and regulation manager. This may result in support to understand how to comply or it may be proposed that a condition or conditions attach to the registration in order to reduce the risks involved in the continued non-compliance.

* If that does not resolve the issues, the process can be escalated to the **National Registration and Enforcement Panel** to ensure that compliance is achieved, depending on the risk to the children in the setting.

* Where the service has failed to address the non-compliance issues at this stage then **removal of the service** from the Register will be considered if there are reasonable grounds to believe that there is a significant risk to the safety, health or welfare of children. This decision can be appealed to Tusla or to the District Court.

In preparation for inspection or as part of an ongoing quality assurance process within a setting it is useful to see the format of an inspection and what a report consists of. The inspection tool used by Tusla can be downloaded from its website and will inform the ongoing oversight of a setting towards full compliance.

Where the Tusla tool is used it will inform the setting about the robustness of the individual policies that are required under the Child Care Act 1991 (Early Years Services) Regulations 2016, and specifically the following policies that are legally required under Schedule 6:

* **Statement of purpose and function** of the setting to inform practice and approaches – values, mission and approaches

* **Complaints procedure** – recording of complaints, procedures and timelines for response, copy retention and resolution procedures

* **Policy on administration of medication** – limits to medicine that will be administered, signatures to allow administration and to record it, procedures to ensure that proper dispensary procedures are followed, recorded and witnessed

* **Policy on infection control** – when children should stay home, how infection will be prevented (this includes Covid-19 measures to be followed in the case of infection)

* **Policy on managing behaviour** – ensuring that children understand what good behaviour is, how it is supported and actions to promote good behaviour and deal with behavioural issues if they arise

* **Policy on safe sleep** – ensuring that everybody understands the value of sleep, the procedures to ensure that children are safe and receive adequate sleep in the setting and procedural responses to requests from parents for sleep to be withheld

* **Fire safety policy** – everybody should be included in the fire safety policy, which extends to safe fire-resistant equipment, escape plans, fire alarms, regular fire drills and other safety measures

* **Inclusion policy** – ensuring that all are welcome in the setting and are facilitated to reach their best potential; it should include any anti-bias measures that are needed

* **Outings policy** – ensuring lists, recording, permissions, procedures, equipment, venues and safe return procedures are followed

* **Policy on accidents and incidents** – what happens if there is an incident in relation to any child; reporting procedures and actions to be followed

* **Policy on authorisation to collect children** – knowing who and when, ensuring the right people only can collect and recording the wishes and instructions in this matter

* **Policy on healthy eating** – nutritious and healthy approaches which support the welfare and wellbeing of the children in the setting, allergies and cultural influences on healthy eating for each child

* **Policy on outdoor play** – equipment, location, duration, protection and inclusion of outdoor play and developmental activities every day

* **Policy on staff absences** – notice, replacement, ratios, returns and ensuring that adequately trained substitutes are available

* **Policy on use of the internet and photographic and recording devices** – ensuring the safety and privacy of children, awareness of potential for harm and procedures to ensure ongoing safe use of equipment, time limits, etc.

* **Settling-in policy** – one of the first policies that parents should be made familiar with; initiation visits with parents, frequency, protection of other children and the inclusion of siblings already in the setting

* **Staff training policy** – ensuring training is available, relevant, resourced and funded, recorded and responsive to the needs and goals of staff in the setting

* **Risk management policy** – where the risks are, how they are to be mitigated, who is responsible and what procedure is used to highlight potential harm

* **Staff supervision** – as discussed earlier in this book (see page 23)

* **Service record retention timeframe** – guided by GDPR and the needs of the setting and incidents which may have arisen within the setting – proportionality, length, purpose and procedure

Sample templates of policies are available in Tusla's *Quality and Regulatory Framework* (QRF).

Everybody has a part to play in implementing good practices and procedures in the setting. Inspectors will be looking at actions and interactions as they go about their inspection process, but compliance should be ongoing and embedded in the approaches used by all staff in the setting under the guidance of the supervisor. While oversight is a management process, implementation involves everyone, every day and in every aspect of their work.

CORRECTIVE AND PREVENTIVE ACTIONS (CAPA)

As outlined above, a CAPA form (see sample in Appendix 6) is issued following the identification by a Tusla inspection of non-compliance with regulatory requirements under the Child Care Act 1991 (Early Years Services) Regulations 2016. It requires the registered provider to address all instances of non-compliance identified during the inspection process.

In a CAPA form, **corrective action** is the action or actions taken to rectify or eliminate the non-compliance identified in the inspection. **Preventive action** relates to ongoing action or actions taken to ensure that the non-compliance will not happen again.

CAPA forms must be typed and must be submitted (by email) within ten working days of receiving the inspection report that the non-compliances were recorded in. They **must be accompanied** by evidence that the non-compliance has been dealt with, e.g. a revised policy or procedure, or photographic evidence of repairs or alterations.

The form must be signed by the registered provider, who is ultimately taking responsibility for the actions being signed off on. The supervisor may be involved in overseeing and ensuring that all staff are involved in rectifying the regulatory breach if it is one where policies or procedures need to be reviewed, but they do not sign the CAPA form.

You will see that the CAPA form uses the SMART approach in relation to corrective and preventive actions. SMART actions are:

* **S**pecific – there must be a specific goal. Tusla directs you to consider six questions:
    1. Who is involved?
    2. What do you want to achieve?
    3. Where will it happen?
    4. When will it happen? Establish a specific timescale.
    5. Which? Identify constraints or requirements needed.
    6. Why? Give specific reasons, purposes or benefits of succeeding.

* **M**easurable – If you know what has to be done you can achieve it, and you will know what is entailed in getting the job done.

* **A**chievable – Identify ways it can happen; look at what skills are needed, who can make it happen and include them in the process.

* **R**ealistic – Make sure you are willing, able and armed appropriately to get it done.

* **T**imely – There is a timeframe to get the job done

The CAPA form asks for a timeframe for actions to happen, and compliance must be achieved within the timeframe outlined to ensure that registration is not affected.

Early Years Education Inspections (EYEIs)

An Early Years Education Inspection (EYEI) is primarily carried out to comply with Section 13 (3) (b) of the Education Act 1988. EYEIs relate to children in the ECCE scheme, and co-operation with these inspections is a condition of the grant agreement for ECCE funding.

An EYEI is designed to:

* Highlight the importance of high-quality early education and care in nurturing the foundations for lifelong learning and in helping children develop to their full potential now and into the future

* Identify and affirm good educational provision in early years settings

* Support the ongoing development of quality in early years settings through the provision of support and advice to practitioners about how children's learning experiences and achievements can be developed or improved

* Complement other national measures to support improvement in early education provision, for example, mentoring and training to support settings provided by Better Start and Aistear/Síolta Practice Guide

* Support self-evaluation and review processes in early years settings

* Provide an assurance of the quality of the early education experienced by children participating in the ECCE programme

* Provide information to the public, including parents of pre-school children, on the quality of education in early years settings through the publication of written inspection reports. (DES 2018)

MODELS OF EYEI INSPECTION

There are two models of inspection: the inspection itself and a follow-through inspection.

The four key principles of EYEI inspections are:

* A focus on learners
* Development and improvement
* Respectful engagement
* Responsibility and accountability.

THE EYEI INSPECTION PROCESS

Before an inspection takes place the DoE Inspectorate liaises with Tusla's Early Years Inspectorate to ensure that there is no overlap, as far as is practicable.

* Settings normally get advance notice (usually two working days) of an inspection.
* However, the DoE Inspectorate can conduct inspections without notice where this is deemed necessary.
* For the most part, documents such as policies are not the focus of these inspections, but they may also be inspected.
* The setting's approaches to learning are the focus of the inspection and documents to support learning processes, planning and routines could be reasonably expected to be examined.
* Meetings are held with all parties in the setting, including the board of management/management committee, staff team and management teams.
* Observations of learning activities are carried out.
* The learning environments (indoors and outdoors) are reviewed.
* Interactions between children and staff are observed.
* Available learning records and documents are reviewed.

AFTER THE INSPECTION

* The outcome is aimed at acknowledging good practices, reviewing any quality issues, identifying areas for development and improvement and advising, if necessary, on actions to bring about improvements.
* Those present can respond to the findings at a feedback meeting at which '**actions advised**' are produced.

* Following the feedback meeting the EYEI report, after details have been verified, is issued to the setting for a **setting response**. The setting can respond with a written response on how they will address the actions advised in the report. The final report will then be published on the DoE website: https://www.gov.ie/en/publication/635fad-early-years-education-inspections/

THE FOLLOW-THROUGH INSPECTION

Underpinned by the same four principles of the EYEI inspection process, this new model of inspection has been recently introduced to the DoE inspection process for early years settings that have already had an EYEI. It looks at the implementation of the actions advised in the initial EYEI report.

Everything about the follow-through inspection is similar to the initial EYEI: two days' notice is given; the structure of the visit also takes a strengths-based approach; and there are pre-inspection/post-inspection meetings. After the inspection, the draft report, factual verification timeframes and publication follow the same processes.

The difference lies in the focus of the follow-through inspection. It looks at progress in implementing specific actions advised, which is categorised as:

* No progress
* Partial progress
* Good progress
* Very good progress.

Funding compliance inspections

Different funding streams in ELC settings have different compliance inspection procedures.

The application process for the funding usually specifies the details that will be the subject of compliance inspections. Documentation required to qualify for the funding streams usually dictate the necessary detail to qualify for the funding and this will differ depending on the needs and expected outcomes of the funding.

Examples of funding streams include (but are not confined to):

* Early Childhood Care and Education (ECCE) Programme
* National Childcare Scheme (NCS)
* Training and Employment Childcare (TEC)
* Community Childcare Subvention Programme (CCSP).

Signing up for any of these initiatives involves contractual obligations. Settings must meet their contractual provisions or they will be deemed to be non-compliant and may be refused funding or may even be liable to refund financial grants already given.

Hive (the early years funding portal) and **PIP** (programme implementation platform) are two platforms that assist in ensuring compliance with a setting's funding requirements. Settings should be familiar with the procedures involved in any inspection process associated with the measures they have applied for. Relevant evidence should be available in an individual setting's compliance folder, as outlined in the funding stream. Pobal is the contracted inspection operator on behalf of the DCEDIY for funding streams, and Pobal visits and inspect to ensure transparency and compliance (Pobal 2020).

FOCUS OF THE COMPLIANCE INSPECTION

The correct use and application of the funding received will be the focus of a compliance visit, which may or may not be announced. The visiting officer (VO) will look at:

* The number of programmes operating

* The number of children registered on the programmes

* The method of record keeping

* The timing of the visit in relation to the cycle of the scheme being funded

* The number of records to be reviewed.

After the inspection, the inspector will go through their findings with the staff member involved in the process and the staff member will be asked to electronically sign the VO's record.

OUTCOMES OF COMPLIANCE VISITS

There are several possible outcomes from a visit:

* Compliant

* Minor non-compliant

* Moderate non-compliant

* Major non-compliant

The overall aim of the process is to ensure that remedial actions are taken to correct any non-compliances identified.

Funding streams provide compliance checklists for providers and it is anticipated that this should eliminate the potential for non-compliance in relation to the details of the VO's inspection (Pobal 2020).

Extend Your Learning

Investigate the following programmes and initiatives, comparing the details in each, and make a comparison list of the rules for each funding initiative:

* ECCE

* AIM

* LINC

Explain how a setting can prepare for inspection under each funding initiative.

Recap

1. **What does 'transparent governance' mean in relation to Tusla inspections?**

2. **What inspections can take place in ELC settings?**

3. **What is a CAPA form?**

4. **Name any nine policies that Tusla inspect.**

5. **Name the four categories of the follow-through inspection model.**

6. **Name the four potential outcomes of a compliance visit.**

7. **What is Hive and how does it help an ELC setting?**

References and further reading

DES (Department of Education and Skills) (2018) *A Guide to Early Years Education Inspection (EYEI)*. Dublin: DES

Pobal (2020) *Compliance Guide for Service Providers – ECCE*. Dublin: DCEDIY

Tusla (2021) *A Guide to Inspection in Early Years Services*. Dublin: Tusla, the Child and Family Agency

Section 4

Relationships

Communication, Partnerships and Collaboration

Learning Goals

In this chapter, learners will:

* Re-examine the legislation around children's rights

* Explore the concept of tri-party working in ELC settings

* Explore the concept of building partnerships in ELC settings

* Learn about the key person approach in ELC

Introduction

The success of any setting is founded on its ability to create and maintain partnerships within and without the setting. For settings in Ireland, the specific protections for children in our Constitution are significant. Those same protections are the basis of the relational practices in every ELC setting.

Children's constitutional rights

Article 42 of the Constitution (Bunreacht na hÉireann) reads as follows:

> "The State acknowledges that the primary and natural educator of the child is the Family and guarantees to respect the inalienable right and duty of parents to provide, according to their means, for the religious and moral, intellectual, physical and social education of their children."

This article impacts on ELC settings as everyone within the setting must uphold the constitutional rights of the child and this means that when they work with any child they do so *in loco parentis* (in the place of the parent). This does not mean that they undertake the responsibilities of the parent, but that they are required to acknowledge parents' rights as the protector of the child.

It is within this framework that we now examine the necessity for, quality of and supports for working in partnership with parents in the interests of their children.

UN Convention on the Rights of the Child (UNCRC)

The rights of children in all states that have committed to the UNCRC are to be protected as human rights. Specific articles in the UNCRC reinforce the need for children's rights to be protected:

* Article 2 – Children cannot be discriminated against.

* Article 3 – Children are entitled to protection and care as necessary for their wellbeing. Institutions, services and facilities responsible for the care or protection of children will conform to standards established by competent authorities. Those standards apply particularly in the areas of safety, health, in the number and suitability of their staff, as well as competent supervision.

* Article 12 – Children have the right to have their views heard in matters relating to them in accordance with their age and maturity.

Both the Constitution and the UNCRC therefore support the requirement that those with children are charged with ensuring that the child's fundamental rights are upheld, without discrimination; that those who work with children do so in the place of those children's parents; and that children's voices should be heard.

Tri-party working in ELC

What we see then is a tri-party working relationship in ELC settings as defined by both the Constitution and the UNCRC (see Figure 13.1).

Childcare staff	Parents/guardians	The child
• Work *in loco parentis* • Must work in partnership	• The custodians of the child's rights and protections	• Entitled to protection • Have the right to have their voice heard

Figure 13.1 The tri-party working relationship in ELC

When parents select the ELC setting for their child they must bear in mind their own responsibility and duty to ensure that the best interests of their child are met and that their development and learning is supported while they are in the ELC setting.

In ELC settings the concept of this working partnership approach is framed within the National Quality Framework for Early Childhood Education (Síolta):

✳ **Standard 3 Parents and Families** promotes processes of formal and informal communication with parents and ensures that parents are involved in their child's care and education within ELC

✳ **Standard 4 Consultation** – promotes the process of communication in relation to the developmental needs, accomplishments and potential challenges the child may have

✳ **Standard 12 Communication** – focuses on the importance of ongoing effective communication with parents in an atmosphere of respect and confidentiality.

The Early Childhood Curriculum Framework (Aistear) also encourages the sharing of observations and assessments with parents in a collaborative way, which is grounded in the ongoing development of a quality workforce whose increased qualification level has enhanced the confidence of practitioners to share information and support a mutual development of informed supports for each child.

Both Aistear and Síolta aim to create a supportive shield for children in the ELC setting. They acknowledge the benefits of a partnership approach for improving the quality of experiences of families in ELC settings.

✳ **Children** feel supported and protected and are consulted on matters that relate to them; they are given opportunities to question actions and decisions others make for them, and to direct actions that will support their awareness of their own needs and wishes.

✳ **Parents** are given meaningful information that will support their child and the child's development and learning. They become active partners and contribute with ELC staff to scaffolding the learning of their child and are better placed to help the child's structured attainment of independence and confidence. They can feel empowered to share more details about the child they know and live with, which can help to align the parent's plans and goals for the child with the activities of the setting.

✳ **Practitioners** develop their pedagogic practices with those who are most affected by them. They share in a process that they are partnering in and they develop their own learning in the process.

Partnerships can also involve others who engage with the child, such as speech and language therapists, physical therapists, etc. The skills of each professional and their interactions with each other will enhance the understanding and the support all professionals can give the child and their family.

Partnership strategies

Ensuring the ongoing involvement of parents in their children's development and learning requires that partnership is facilitated, reflected and mirrored in meaningful ways so that parents can engage with the process whatever their circumstances. An ELC setting should ensure that information is readily accessible in order to ensure engagement in partnership-building which can be effected in several ways, as shown in Figure 13.2. The opportunities are boundless and the outcomes countless.

Figure 13.2 Partnership-building strategies in ELC

THE KEY PERSON APPROACH

For young children, settling into an ELC setting can be strange, upsetting and a source of anxiety. This can be mitigated by putting in place a key person strategy. This involves assigning each child a particular educator who builds a special relationship with the child and acts as a primary contact with the parents in support of the child.

The key person approach has several benefits:

* It supports an individual and focused relationship with the child, which can alleviate anxiety and stress.

* The key person closely interacts with that child and can notice developments or changes more quickly.

* It facilitates partnership conversations; an ongoing relationship that is visible and supportive may make interactions easier for parents when issues arise.

* Parents will be supported by the idea that the key person is their go-to person.

THINK AND REFLECT

1   Design a newsletter for parents that explains the importance of partnership in an ELC setting and how it can be promoted.

2   Consider how you might support parents when their child is about to leave the ELC setting and start primary school. What activities and approaches would you use? How would you introduce them?

Practitioner/parent structures

Supervisors who recognise and promote the importance of effective partnership approaches within their settings will establish support structures to ensure that the communication within the setting is open, honest, frank and reflective. The supervision process itself will ensure that staff feel enabled, informed, trained and confident about engaging with parents in particular so that they can learn more and teach more about the needs, abilities, styles of learning and achieving milestones for the children they work with. The partnership processes implemented and modelled in the ELC setting underpin the foundation of children's learning throughout lifelong learning journeys. They demonstrate to the child that they are part of a network of people who support, encourage, enable and nuture, and who have their best interests at the centre of everything they do.

The importance of partnership, support, valuing the rights of children and working in their best interests is recognised in the Code of Professional Responsibilities and Code of Ethics for Early Years Educators developed by the Professionalisation Sub-Group of the Early Years Forum (the term 'early years educator' refers to ELC practitioners):

" 1. The child's individuality, strengths, needs and rights are central in the provision of quality early childhood education and care settings. Children have the right to be listened to and appropriately responded to.

2. Parents are the primary educators of the young child and have a pre-eminent role in promoting her/his health, wellbeing, learning and development. Open, honest and respectful partnership with parents is essential in promoting the best interests of the child. Implicit to this is the need to support parents and families in that role.

3. Positive relationships, which are secure, responsive and respectful and which provide consistency and continuity over time, are the cornerstone of the child's wellbeing.

4. Equality, as articulated in Article 2 of the UN Convention on the Rights of the Child (1989) and in the Equal Status Acts 2000 to 2004, is a fundamental characteristic of quality early childhood care and education provision.

5. Early years educators respect diversity and ensure that all children and families have their individual, personal, cultural and linguistic identity valued.

6. The health, wellbeing, safety, welfare and education of all children must be protected and promoted in all early childhood environments.

7. Early years educators understand the role of play as central to the wellbeing, development and learning of the young child.

8. Throughout childhood, care and education are inseparable and early years educators express this by curricula or programmes of activities which take a holistic approach to the development and learning of the young child.

9. Early years educators value training and professional qualifications and participate in continuous professional development. They will assist students of early years teaching in their learning.

10. In seeking to respond to the needs of young children, early years educators will seek to involve other professionals and agencies as appropriate.

11. Early years educators, having taken into account the rights of others, will provide service users with full information, including access to records pertaining to work on their behalf.

12. Early years educators will act with responsibility, accountability and integrity at all times. Early years educators should be prepared to reflect on and state the reasons for their practice and decisions.

13. Early years educators will respect a service user's right to confidentiality. It is the duty of the early years educator to ensure that the nature and limits of the privacy inherent in their relationship are clearly understood and applied.

14. Early years educators actively promote children's citizenship in their local, regional and national communities. "

BARNARDO'S PARTNERSHIP WITH PARENTS (PWP) PROGRAMME

Several Barnardos publications support the concept of working in partnership with families, and Barnardos has developed a unique resource and procedural strategy called Partnership with Parents (PwP), which addresses issues that arise with families in many different situations. It is a valuable resource for any setting considering implementing a partnership approach (Barnardos 2013). One evaluation of this programme highlights the value of such an approach for children, parents and families (Connolly *et al.* 2019).

The services offered by this programme include:

* Practical support
* Behaviour approaches
* Social development
* Routine support
* Education
* Physical development advice
* Crisis management support.

The results of this programme are shown in Figure 13.3.

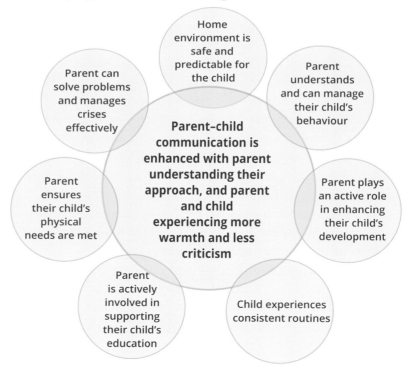

Figure 13.3 Outcomes of Partnership with Parents (adapted from PwP logic model (Barnardos, 2013))

TUSLA'S PREVENTION, PARTNERSHIP AND FAMILY SUPPORT (PPFS) PROGRAMME

Tusla's Prevention, Partnership and Family Support (PPFS) programme (Tusla 2013) takes a supportive approach to enabling families and parents to develop their coping skills where challenges are evident by:

* Supporting the participation of children in decisions that affect them

* Supporting parents in developing parenting skills

* Adopting a new approach to commissioning, starting with commissioning parenting support

* Implementing area-based prevention and early intervention approaches through Child and Family Support Networks and Meitheal

* Raising awareness of programmes to support families and communities.

FIRST 5

More recently, the focus of the government's First 5 Implementation Plan (Government of Ireland 2019) on the requirement to work and support families and children through those interactions that determine a child's future development included, as its 5 Big Steps:

* Access to a broader range of options for parents to balance working and caring

* A new model of parenting support

* New developments in child health

* Reform of the Early Learning and Care (ELC) system

* A package of measures to tackle early childhood poverty.

First 5 and parental involvement

First 5 seeks to embrace and build on the strands in the PPFS and PwP, as shown in Strategic Action 7.2:

> **"**Strategic Action 7.2: Facilitate and encourage greater parental involvement and engagement in early learning in ELC settings and primary schools.
>
> 7.2 Initial Actions
>
> — Develop guidance and information for parents and families on ELC (and school-age childcare), including information on ELC (and school-age childcare) options and entitlements and guidance on key indicators of high-quality provision. Over time, explore the potential to develop a real-time finder of regulated ELC (and school-age childcare) places with links to inspection reports and other relevant information.

> — Support greater parental involvement and engagement in children's early learning in ELC settings and primary schools.
>
> — Develop advice, guidance and training for ELC settings and primary schools to build effective working relationships with all parents, families and communities.
>
> — Support ELC settings and primary schools to create opportunities to encourage and strengthen involvement of parents such as parent–practitioner meetings, parental advisory boards, home–ELC liaison officers, designated staff with responsibility for supporting parents, including initiatives in collaboration with the National Parents' Council (Pre-Primary and Primary). "

The structures that every supervisor oversees in the ELC setting will need to be focused on the strategic goals and plans within First 5.

What is very clear in these developments and programmes is an identification of the need for meaningful interactions, supports and structures in the relationship between ELC practitioners and parents to support positive working strategies that will be informed by ongoing ELC structures, research, education and training for all practitioners, supported by regulation and inspection. This is a developing and changing focus on the work of practitioners in ELC.

Facilitating children's voices

Having their voices heard in everything they are involved in is a child's human right and is underwritten by the United Nations Convention on the Rights of the Child (UNCRC). Ensuring that the voice of the child is heard is foundational to the ELC practices envisaged in:

* Síolta, the National Quality Framework (2006) – currently being revised

* Aistear, the Early Childhood Curriculum Framework (2009) – currently being revised

* Child Care Act 1991 (Early Years Services) Regulations 2016

* Diversity, Equality and Inclusion Charter and Guidelines (2016)

* First 5 Implementation Plan 2019–2021

A number of initiatives have been supported by government as part of its legal requirement to ensure that the voice of the child is heard in proportion to their age and stage of development as outlined specifically in Article 12 of the UNCRC. Some of these initiatives are shown in Figure 13.4.

Lundy Model
Creative Schools
Comhairle na nÓg
Ombudsman for Children
National Youth Council of Ireland
AIM (Access and Inclusion Model)
LINC (Leadership in Inclusivity)
Síolta Quality Framework
Aistear Curriculum Framework

Figure 13.4 Voice of the child initiatives

What is clear is that there is a focus on including the best interests of the child, facilitating their inclusion in our society at all levels, and an ongoing commitment to ensuring that children of all ages are assisted to develop as enabled citizens who will participate according to their age and stage of maturity.

THINK AND REFLECT 🍃

Investigate two of the initiatives that aim to ensure that the voice of the child is heard. Present your findings in a digital format that others in your group can add to and create a learning resource for others.

Recap

1. **What is the name of the agreement that ensures that children's voices are heard in matters that relate to them?**

2. **What does PPFS stand for?**

3. **Explain why partnership is important in ELC.**

4. **Name five government-supported initiatives in Ireland that support the child's right to have their voice heard.**

References and further reading

Aistear (2009) *The Early Childhood Curriculum Framework*. Dublin: NCCA

Barnardos (2013) *Partnership with Parents Manual*. Dublin: Barnardos

Barnardos (2019) *Evaluation of the Partnership with Parents Programme*. Dublin: Barnardos

Connolly, N., Adams, K. and Fleming, P. (2019) *Evaluation of the Partnership with Parents Programme*. Dublin: Barnardos

Department of Health (2000) *National Children's Strategy: Our Children – Their Lives*. Dublin: Stationery Office

Government of Ireland (2018) *First 5: A Government Strategy for Babies, Young Children and their Families, 2019–2028*. Dublin: Stationery Office

Government of Ireland (2019) *First 5 Implementation Plan 2019–2021* Dublin: Stationery Office

Síolta (2006) *Siolta: the National Quality Framework*. Dublin: NCCA

Support Structures, Research and Developments

Learning Goals

In this chapter, learners will:

* Learn about Pobal, its role and function in the ELC sector

* Examine the concept of ECCE

* Learn about how AIM works

* Look at some funding structures in the constantly changing ELC sector

Introduction

We have mentioned several government-funded programmes throughout this book. All are designed to make sure that the children you will care for in your ELC setting and the staff you supervise will be supported in their development. In the case of those you supervise there is a development support structure emerging that will ensure that they are well qualified for the tasks they undertake; they will have clear progression paths through their career; they will take a professional approach to the work they do; and they will be clear about the immense benefits they bring to the ELC sector.

For the children you work with, the developments and programmes will ensure that those children are aware of their abilities, will be supported in adding their own voice to the processes that surround and support them, and will contribute to their becoming lifelong learners. They will see positive role models and learn in child-focused ways and will see that their parents are part of the structures and processes in

ELC settings. Their needs will be the focus of the supporting structures that envelop their development and they will be encouraged to learn in whatever style they are best suited to or ready for, and this will be informed by wider pedagogical approaches in the developing ELC sector, including school-age childcare (SAC). This will bring a uniformity to the combined sector but, more important, will also create robust structures that assist every child throughout the country to reach their best potential, as is their human right.

Pobal

Pobal is a non-profit company that operates under the aegis of the Department of Rural and Community Development (Indecon 2021). It provides management, support and fund administration for a number of other government departments and agencies.

As summarised in the recent Indecon review, its key functions in relation to ELC and SAC are shown in Figure 14.1.

1. Provides oversight of ELC and SAC funding programmes

2. Engages in compliance, audit and risk oversight of ELC and SAC funding programmes

3. Provides CCC (City/County Childcare Committees) and NCVO (National Council of Voluntary Organisations) budgetary management

4. Carries out verification visits to CCCs to assess programme expenditure

5. Highlights to DCEDIY any concerns raised by CCC in relation to their Statement of Work

6. Assesses the performance of CCCs by appraising and monitoring the local planning and implementation of activities and outcomes

7. Works in collaboration with DCEDIY and CCCs on the case management process to assess and support ELC services in difficulty

8. Oversees development and agreement on the annual Performance Delivery Agreement for the NCS (National Childcare Scheme) and Programme of Work for other early years programmes

9. Responsible for the management and enhancement of the Early Years Programme and Hive

Figure 14.1 A summary of Pobal's functions

Under the proposals of the Indecon review, which have already informed the planning of supports and structures for the amalgamation of ELC and SAC, the functions and operations of Pobal may change in the near future. We shall not examine those proposals in this book, but it is an area to keep abreast of.

Programmes of support

Each programme of support has different aims and different rules. Some you will be very familiar with; others you may not have had the opportunity to implement in your setting. The following is a brief introduction to the main government-funded programmes. You are encouraged to examine the rules for each in your own research journey so that when the need for the programme presents itself, you will know what is involved. Being aware of these programmes will help you to ensure that the children you care for have their needs met in a timely way that will not create developmental delays in their care or education during the fundamental years between ages 0 and 6.

Information on many of the programmes mentioned in this book can be accessed on the Early Years Hive at https://earlyyearshive.ncs.gov.ie/ or by emailing eypc@pobal.ie.

What becomes clear from a summary of some of the initiatives in ELC that will be incorporated into the amalgamation with SAC is that there are overlaps in provision, rules and application which will only become more complicated with the new developments planned as part of First 5's vision for ELC and SAC, and children's care and support commitments already outlined in the First 5 strategy (Government of Ireland 2018).

Early Childhood Care and Education (ECCE) programme

First announced in Budget 2009 and effective since 2010, initially as a one-year scheme, the ECCE programme is now a two-year provision for pre-school children. The scheme provides funding to offer access to pre-school care and education to children in early years settings (pre-schools, Montessori schools, crèches, playgroups) for three hours a day, five days a week, 38 weeks of the year (183 days in total). All children are entitled to two full academic years (September to June) on the ECCE scheme.

Children are eligible to begin the ECCE scheme in the September of the year that they turn 3 years of age but they must have turned 2 years and 8 months before they start. Thus for the current year (2022/2023) the child must have turned 2 years and 8 months on or before 31 August 2022. The scheme is not mandatory and parents can choose whether or not to send their children to ECCE. Where a parent decides to send their child later than the age of 3, they should be no older than 5 years and 6 months on or before June 2022 (for the year 2022/2023) in order to qualify for ECCE funding.

* Pobal administers the ECCE on Hive on behalf of DCEDIY and queries are directed to City/County Childcare Committees (CCCs) in relation to the rules of the scheme.

* The ELC Service Provider must be a limited company **or** a designated activity company (DAC) **or** a sole trader **or** a school board of management **or** a not-for-profit organisation **or** a partnership – in other words there must be some legally recognised business structure to the service provider.

* The service must be registered with Tusla to receive funding from DCEDIY.

* All facilities provided must be registered with Tusla and have an Individual Service Reference Number.

* Children must only attend an ECCE scheme they are registered for.

* ECCE service providers must administer their ECCE scheme on Hive (see www.pobal.ie).

* There must be a funding agreement in place.

* A list of fees and service charges must be agreed in advance through Hive and this list must provide details of any deposit required, discounts allowed and additional optional extra charges.

* ECCE operators receive a capitation fee from DCEDIY and cannot charge for anything else whatsoever.

* Staff must have a minimum QQI Level 5 qualification.

* Higher capitation (an extra €11.25 per child above the current rate of €69 standard rate) is offered for services where:

  — The room leader has a Level 7 qualification

  — The same room leader has a minimum of three years' (three full academic years, which excludes practice placements) paid experience working in the childcare sector

  — The child:carer ratio is being met

  — Room assistants in the ECCE room (where required by the ratios) hold a minimum QQI Level 5 qualification.

Access and Inclusion Model (AIM)

This is a model of supports specifically designed to ensure that children with disabilities can access the ECCE programme, so it is embedded within the ECCE service. The goal of AIM is to enable ELC providers to deliver an inclusive pre-school experience that all eligible children can assess and benefit from.

AIM is specifically designed as a child-centred model of provision and involves seven levels of progressive supports, ranging from universal level to targeted level, based on the need of the child and the pre-school service. Tailored supports are based on the need assessed and a formal diagnosis of disability for the child is not required.

In order to qualify for AIM a child must be registered for a specific ECCE setting so that the matching of need and supports resulting from those identified needs can then be properly tailored to the specifics of the child and the ECCE setting.

* Because AIM is embedded in the ECCE scheme the qualifying age criteria of ECCE applies to AIM.

* There is no need for the child to have an assessment of disability and a formal diagnosis of disability will not guarantee additional AIM supports as it may be decided that the setting's supports are sufficient.

* The definition of disability for AIM differs from that of the Disability Act 2005 and is 'a long-term physical, mental, intellectual or sensory impairment which, in interaction with various barriers may hinder a child's full and effective participation in society on an equal basis with others'.

* AIM is designed around a number of levels which do not refer to the level of disability of the child but to the levels or support offered by the scheme:

  — Level 1 – the ELC setting can participate in the LINC programme (Leadership for Inclusion in Early Years) Level 6 Special Purpose Award provided by Mary Immaculate College, Limerick. An extra €2 is currently provided to providers under Level 1.

  — Level 2 – the provision of accurate and up-to-date information about AIM for parents and providers.

  — Level 3 – training and education for the workforce; refers to the provision of three free CPD courses:

    — Hanen – training to help ELC settings enable children to develop language and literacy skills

    — Lámh – an Irish sign language system for adults and children with intellectual disability and communication needs

    — SPEL – Sensory Processing E-Learning programme.

— Level 4 – provides access to early years specialists delivered under the Better Start service (Early Years Specialist Service (EYSS)), who will provide coaching and mentoring to the ELC staff in the ECCE programme.

— Level 5 – provision of specialist equipment or appliances and capital grants towards minor building adjustments to ensure the child can participate fully (e.g. ramps, hoists, etc.) and free training on using the equipment.

— Level 6 – provides HSE therapeutic supports, including behaviour support plans and professional advice.

— Level 7 – provides additional funding for the setting which can be used either to reduce the child:adult ratio in the ECCE room or to fund an extra staff member as a shared resource in the ECCE room.

There are systems to verify the level of supports offered under AIM. For instance, for a Level 7 classification:

* Recommendation by a Better Start early years specialist (who may visit or conduct a service observation review (SOR)) to determine whether Level 7 support is needed

* Review of application by appraisal officer in Pobal

* Final decision by deciding officer in Pobal.

AIM is based on the concept of Universal Design for Early Learning and Care Settings and supports the knowledge base of settings in providing for children with disabilities or AIM classification levels as they register for ECCE programmes.

Current funding structures

The current structural supports for the ELC sector are divided between a number of organisations overseen by DCEDIY. Additionally, the Department of Education has support and oversight involvement with ELCs:

* Pobal Early Years

* Compliance Audit and Risk

* Better Start

* National Voluntary Childcare Organisations (NVCOs), of which there are 7

* Childcare Committees Ireland (CCI)

* City and County Childcare Committees (CCC), of which there are thirty

* Tusla

* Tusla Early Years Inspectorate

* Department of Education (DoE)

* National Council for Curriculum and Assessment (NCCA)

* DoE Early Years Inspectorate.

The structure of these processes, while effective, is also cumbersome and can be awkward to navigate. In its recent review Indecon (2021) summarised the responsibilities of some of these organisations:

Summary of functions in ELC

	Policy	Comms	Training	Information	Inspection/ compliance	Advice	Data collection
DCEIDY	Yes	Yes	No	Yes	No	No	Yes
DoE	Yes	Yes	Yes	Yes	Yes	Yes	Yes
Pobal	No	Yes	Yes	Yes	Yes	Yes	Yes
Better Start	No	Yes	Yes	Yes	Yes	Yes	Yes
Tusla	No	Yes	Yes	Yes	Yes	No	Yes
CCC	No	Yes	Yes	Yes	No	Yes	Yes
NVCO	No	Yes	Yes	Yes	No	Yes	Yes

Source: Indecon 2021

This table shows how complicated the current model is.

Indecon also highlighted the strengths and weaknesses of the current structures:

Strengths	Weaknesses
Responsibility with one department for the integration of ELC and SAC policies	Concerns over the ability of the current system to handle the scale of reform needed to combine ELC and SAC
Existence of a national strategic policy (First 5)	Fragmentation and duplication with resultant complexities for providers and parents
All the main components to support service provision are in place	Gaps in compliance with best practice governance
Experience and expertise	Accountability concerns due to multiplicity of agencies and providers

Strengths	Weaknesses
Agility of support structures in adjusting to changing requirements	Insufficient public management or private provision/inconsistency in level of supply
Local knowledge	Concern over ownership and management of assets funded by Exchequer
Commitment to continuous improvement	Impact on department undertaking significant operational activities
Investment in research and evaluation	Absence of shared services to support sole suppliers

Source: Indecon 2021

Keeping up to date

Even from this brief introduction to the schemes and structures in the ELC sector and the changing nature of planned implementations it is obvious that a big part of the responsibility of a supervisor in ELC is keeping up to date with changes within the sector as they arise.

Some research is disseminated by organisations such as Early Childhood Ireland (ECI), which represents those who are involved in the ELC sector at provision level. ECI makes available updates to regulations, updates to funding streams and other policy developments in the ELC sector and is a very valuable resource for any supervisor to have access to. Additional updates are available from the Hive resource and this is a highly useful ally in identifying and understanding funding streams for the ELC and SAC sector.

Other sources of research and information on wider aspects of development and change in ELC and SAC include:

* DCEDIY – www.dcediy.ie

* Economic and Social Research Institute (ESRI) – www.esri.ie

* OECD – www.oecd.ie

* Oireachtas Committee reports – www.oireachtas.ie

There are also opportunities to partake in research that will inform planning. The Indecon review notes that many of the developments that are taking place will be studied by those who are emerging from training in colleges of further and higher education. Supporting the learning of those on placement/practicums from college will enhance the level of knowledge in the individual ELCs they are attached to, and that supports the growth of knowledge of everyone in ELC.

Recap

1. **What are the functions of Pobal?**

2. **Name some of the organisations currently involved in ELC funding.**

3. **Outline three differences between the ECCE scheme and the AIM scheme.**

4. **Where might you find detailed information about research on the ELC sector?**

5. **Explore four organisations that you could subscribe to in order to keep up to date with developments in the ELC sector. Complete the subscription process for those four organisations.**

References and further reading

Government of Ireland (2018) *First 5: A Government Strategy for Babies, Young Children and their Families, 2019–2028*. Dublin: Stationery Office

Indecon (2021) *Review of Early Learning and Care ('ELC') and School Age Childcare ('SAC') Operating Model in Ireland*. Dublin: Indecon International Consultants, for DCEDIY

Appendices

Appendix 1 Sample Staff Supervision Policy

(See www.tusla.ie)

This can also be called a Staff Support and Supervision Policy, as support is an inherent part of professional supervision.

1 RATIONALE AND POLICY CONSIDERATIONS

The Staff Supervision Policy in relation to an early years service means a policy specifying the way employees, unpaid workers and contractors are supervised and supported in the service in relation to their work practices.

Staff development provides chances for greater knowledge, improved skill and better understanding, not as an end in itself but as a means to develop and improve the level of service to children and their families. Good supervision can increase reflective practice and research has shown that good supervision is associated with job satisfaction, commitment and staff retention.

Supervision and appraisals are core elements of the staff development process for all team members, paid or unpaid. Team meetings and mentoring also form part of a quality support and supervision, and a team development structure for the staff team.

The purpose of supervision is to provide support to team members as well as to promote and provide accountability for work practice. Good supervision supports decision-making, development of the work and development of the staff member's knowledge, skills and competencies.

Appraisals provide an opportunity to acknowledge an individual staff member's strengths and a context for setting new professional development goals. Appraisals also contribute to identifying training and development needs of staff members.

LEGISLATION AND REGULATORY REQUIREMENTS

* Under Regulation 9 of the Child Care Act 1991 (Early Years Services) Regulations 2016 the registered provider must ensure that staff are appropriately supervised in relation to all the regulatory requirements for the service.

* Having a clear, written policy and procedure on staff supervision is a requirement under Regulation 10 of the Child Care Act 1991 (Early Years Services) Regulations 2016.

CHILDREN'S NEEDS

Children need:

* To be cared for and educated by adults who are well supported in their role and whose practice is monitored to ensure that the care and education they receive while attending the service is of good quality

* The adults, whose role is to work alongside their parents/guardians, in supporting their wellbeing, learning and development, to be encouraged and supported to be reflective practitioners and to feel valued in this very important and significant role.

PARENTS'/FAMILIES' NEEDS

Parents/guardians need to know that:

* The service provided for their child's learning and development is of a high quality

* Staff to whom they entrust their young child's care and education, while in the service, are adequately and appropriately informed, motivated, supported, guided and monitored in their role.

STAFF NEEDS

Staff members need:

* This policy to ensure that they will be appropriately supported in their very important role

* To be able to discuss the day-to-day issues, challenges and opportunities that inevitably come with providing quality care and education to young children and interacting with their parents/guardians

* A safe space in which to be able to address any potential challenges associated with interacting positively at all times with their colleagues

* To be accountable for the quality of their practice

* To be given information that relates to their position in the service, in an appropriate context, and be able to rely on having specific time dedicated to their particular support needs, by their manager.

MANAGEMENT NEEDS

Management needs:

* To ensure that they meet the requirements of the Early Years Regulations in relation to how support and supervision of employees, unpaid workers and contractors, relating to their work practices, are provided.

* To ensure that the service's Supervision Policy is known and understood by all staff members.

* To ensure that the expectations of the service in relation to supervision, and the purpose of supervision, are clear to all staff members.

* The arrangements for support and supervision set out and made clear to all team members and also to parents/guardians who use the service.

NATIONAL QUALITY FRAMEWORKS

* Tusla: Quality and Regulatory Framework

* Síolta: The National Quality Framework for Early Childhood Education

DEFINITIONS/GLOSSARY

(Include definitions here of any words/phrases used in the policy that may need explanation. For example:)

Supervision	A key managerial activity. It is communication between two or more staff members, one of whom is a line manager, to support and develop the knowledge, skills and values of the staff member/s to help improve outcomes for the children and families who use the service and the staff member/s themselves – it is a formal reflective process about professional thinking, actions and decisions (Social Care Institute for Excellence (www.scie.org.uk))
Appraisals	A formal process in which the work and professional development of an individual staff member are reviewed. The process acknowledges the worker's strengths and contributes to future planning and goal-setting. Appraisals are about a person's previous performance and future development. The appraisal considers the staff member's achievements, their expectations, and their training and development needs.

2 POLICY STATEMENT

(Outlines the principles, values and purpose of the policy. It will generally be quite short.)

All staff members must have a regular, consistent and uninterrupted supervision meeting with their **supervisor/manager** based on a negotiated agreement to:

* Support them in their work

* Ensure that they are clear about their role and responsibilities

* Ensure competent and accountable performance

* Ensure that, in their respective roles, they meet [service name] standards and objectives

* Ensure a positive atmosphere for practice

* Support their professional development

* Help keep stress to a minimum

* Increase awareness of new areas of professional knowledge

* Ensure that they are given the resources to do their job

* Provide an opportunity to voice their ideas and concerns

* Ensure the quality of service provided to children and families.

Staff members are encouraged to reflect on the quality of their practice, continuously update their knowledge base and raise any safeguarding concerns.

Staff members will be supported appropriately in the case of child protection concerns and outside support will be sought if it is needed.

All staff members are entitled to:

* Respect as a person and in their role

* Clarity in relation to their role and responsibilities

* Clarity about the boundaries of confidentiality – where it is necessary to inform others of something that arises during supervision, the supervisor and supervisee should discuss how this can be done

* Clarity about expectations

* Have their experience and contribution acknowledged

* Be briefed about changes in the service

* Participate in planning and problem solving and not just be told what to do

* Access to CPD/training relevant to their job

* Clarification about the service's policies and procedures

* Clear performance targets

* Be allocated an appropriate and manageable workload

* Clarity about the basis of decisions that impact on them either directly or indirectly

* Regular and uninterrupted supervision

* Formal appraisal.

The supervision programme will be reviewed at least annually to ensure that it is effective.

Staff appraisals will be carried out for each staff member within the first six months of appointment and annually thereafter.

3 PROCEDURES AND PRACTICES

(Outlines the specific steps and/or guidance to be followed in order to implement the policy.)

SUPERVISION

Before the first supervision meeting, an initial discussion takes place between supervisor and supervisee to discuss what supervision is and also what it is not, and to outline the frequency, duration and format of supervision meetings. Both participants' expectations are discussed, clarified and agreed at the beginning of the supervision relationship.

A Supervision Meeting will be scheduled [*monthly/every six weeks*], at least [*number*] months in advance, with each staff member (paid or unpaid). [*Outline who in the service will supervise whom – anyone assigned as supervisor must be appropriately trained.*] The meeting will generally be a minimum of one hour's duration. [*Outline when and where supervision takes place and the resources available.*]

There will be an agreed agenda for the meeting.

AREAS FOR DISCUSSION

(Outline the type of areas for discussion within supervision.)

There is likely to be a number of standing items on the agenda for supervision. In an early years educator role, the agenda items may include but are not limited to:

* Care and welfare of the group

* Care and welfare of individual children

* Contact and work with parents/guardians and families/key person role

* Any new ideas/reflections on quality practice

* Any concerns including, but not limited to, child safeguarding concerns

* Networking with other agencies and organisations

* Training needs

* Teamwork

* Staff welfare and support

* Health and safety issues.

RECORDS AND RECORD-KEEPING

The supervision session is recorded by the supervisor and the record kept in accordance with good practice, legislation and regulation in [*where the record will be stored*] (see Record-keeping Policy). Both supervisor and supervisee sign the record to ensure that it is an accurate and fair reflection of the discussion and decisions. Decisions made at one session will be followed up at the next session to ensure they were acted upon.

SUPERVISION OF STUDENTS

Students/trainees who work with the children are at all times under the supervision of an appropriately qualified staff member. They are supported and supervised by appropriately experienced members of staff to assist them to carry out their duties to promote and protect the wellbeing, learning and development of the children.

TEAM MEETINGS

(You can include the service policy guidance on team meetings here and/or in the staff training policy.)

Regular and consistent team meetings are an integral part of team, individual and service development as well as being core to communication within the team. Team meetings can have a number of different functions, including:

* Information sharing

* Decision-making

* Developing the team/teamwork

* Review, reflection, evaluation and planning

* Debriefing and support

* Skills development/sharing knowledge from training attended.

All team meetings and decisions made should be in the interests of the children and families who use the service. Meetings need to have a clear purpose and direction and a clear recorded outcome. There needs to be an agreed agenda, a timeframe, minutes, a chairperson (not necessarily the owner/manager) and open discussion and reflection.

MENTORING AND/OR COACHING

(The service's approach (if any) to mentoring and/or coaching as a form of support and guidance can also be included here and/or in the staff training policy.)

Mentoring and coaching do not involve line management responsibility but are supportive of people and practice. The role of mentor is to provide an opportunity for reflection on work and learn from this. The mentor shares their experience and provides encouragement and support. The mentoring relationship can be formal or informal.

The coaching relationship is more directive – the coach suggests ways of improving practice and skills.

APPRAISALS

All new staff members have an appraisal carried out before the end of their probationary period and annually thereafter.

All staff members' appraisals follow the same format using the service's standard appraisal form.

The following is a list of questions that may be helpful to include when developing your appraisal form. The purpose of the form is to support preparing for and carrying out, as well as recording, an appraisal:

* What have been your achievements during the last year?

* How do these relate to the goals you had at the beginning of the year?

* How do they relate to the service's goals?

* What are your particular strengths in relation to your work here?

* What have you contributed to the team/service?

* What situations/issues have challenged you?

* What has contributed to effective work/practice?

* What has got in the way of effective work?

* What have you learned and what would you like to learn?

* What goals would you like to set for the coming year?

* What do you think the service/your colleagues can do to contribute to you achieving your goals?

Appraisals relate to the individual's job description and focus on areas of performance relevant to their role.

Appraisals are recorded and records kept in each staff member's own personnel file in accordance with good practice and legislation and regulation (see Records and Record-keeping Policy).

Where there is disagreement between the parties, they must, in the first instance, try to resolve issues between themselves in a respectful manner, each listening to the other's point of view. Should this fail and agreement not be reached [*state how the issue will be addressed and by whom, for example intervention by the staff representative of the management committee/a senior manager/a mediator*].

4 COMMUNICATION PLAN

(For staff and families)

Staff members are informed of the policy and procedures regarding Staff Support and Supervision on commencing in the service. The registered provider/person in charge will check with staff members that they have read and understood the policy and provide any assistance needed.

Familiarity with this policy will be included in staff induction and annual staff training.

A copy of all relevant policies will be available during all hours of operation to all staff team members in the policy folder located in _____.

All staff members will receive written notification of any updates.

Parents and guardians are informed that there is a supervision policy and may see it and/or receive a copy of the policy at any time on request.

5 RELATED POLICIES, PROCEDURES AND FORMS

(List of all related documents. The policies in bold are those required under the Early Years Regulations 2016.)

* **Staff Training Policy**
* **Risk Management Policy**
* Records and Record-keeping Policy
* Confidentiality Policy
* Supervision Record Form
* Appraisals Record Form

6 REFERENCES/SUPPORTING DOCUMENTS/ RELATED LEGISLATION

(List any relevant legislation and practice guides referred to in drafting the policy.)

* Tusla: Quality and Regulatory Framework
* Child Care Act 1991 (Early Years Services) Regulations 2016

* Freedom of Information (FOI) Act, 2014

* Data Protection Act, 1988 and 2003

* *Reflective Practice for Early Childhood Professionals* (Barnardos 2015)

* *Human Resource Management in Early Years Services* (Barnardos 2010)

* *Supporting Quality: Guidelines for Professional Practice in Early Childhood Services* (3rd edn), Book 1: *Policy and Governance* (Barnardos 2008)

7 WHO MUST OBSERVE THIS POLICY

This policy must be observed by all managers and all staff members.

Actions to be taken if the policy is not implemented:

(Add any relevant actions to be taken.)

8 CONTACT INFORMATION

If you need more information about this policy, contact:

Name: _____

Phone number: _____

Email: _____

Policy created on [*date*] _____.

Approved by:

Name: _____

Position: _____

Signature: _____

Name: _____

Position: _____

Signature: _____

Date this policy will be reviewed: _____

Appendix 2 Sample Supervision Memorandum of Agreement

This Memorandum outlines the understanding and mutual expectations of both parties in the process of Supervision in _____ Early Learning and Care.

Supervision is agreed between:

Supervisor: _____

and

Supervisee: _____

The key areas to be addressed in supervision are:

1. To enable the Supervisee to comply with the standards specified by the policies and procedures in _____ Early Care and Learning and to comply with Regulation 9 of the Child Care Act 1991 (Early Years Services) Regulations 2016 and Regulation 10 of the Child Care Act 1991 (Early Years Services) Regulations 2016

2. To ensure that the Supervisee is clear about his/her roles and responsibilities and to support the Supervisee in understanding the standards for best practice within _____ Early Learning and Care

3. To ensure accountability and understanding of the work undertaken by the Supervisee with the assistance of the Supervisor

4. To give regular assistance in the process of the worker's professional development with support and feedback that encourages reflection, constructive feedback and resolution of issues and challenges encountered by the Supervisee

5. To be a primary source of support for the Supervisee as they develop professionally

6. To review the supervision contract annually

It is important in the supervision process, and therefore expected, that both Supervisor and Supervisee will prepare for supervision sessions that are arranged as follows:

Frequency (how often sessions will take place)	
Length of time for each session	
Location for supervision sessions	
Method of recording supervision sessions (All records should be signed by both Supervisor and Supervisee and dated at the end of each supervision session)	
Purpose(s) for which the supervisory record may be used *Note:* There may be circumstances when things discussed may need to be brought to the attention of others and this should only be done with prior notice to the Supervisee	
Storage of supervision record (Where it will be stored and who will ensure it is stored correctly)	
If a supervision session is not held/attended, another will be organised within (*Specify a time period and who will organise the rearranged session*)	
How will the agenda for sessions be agreed and who will be responsible for sending the agenda to the other person?	
What is the contribution of and how will we record other supervision events if they arise between sessions?	

Mutual expectations:

What I as the supervisee expect from you as my supervisor:

_____

_____

_____

What I as the supervisor expect from you as my supervisee:

_____

_____

_____

Permissions that we have agreed:
(If the supervisee does not agree with an item, it should be recorded)

_____

_____

_____

_____

What will we do if there are difficulties working together?

_____

_____

_____

_____

Signed (Supervisor): _____

Date: _____

Signed (Supervisee): _____

Date: _____

This Memorandum of Agreement including the content, frequency, length of session, and record-keeping processes will be reviewed on [_at least every year_]:

_____

(Adapted from https://www.hse.ie/eng/about/who/qid/socialcareapplframework/
hse-staff-supervision-policy-eg-child-and-family-agency.pdf)

Appendix 3 Schedule of Supervision Meetings Template

This record should be kept attached to the front of the supervisee's supervision file.

Supervisor's name	
Supervisee's name	
Meeting location	

Scheduled date	Time	Duration of session	Supervisor initials	Supervisee initials	Reminders or rescheduling notes

Appendix 4 Sample Supervision Record Template

This table should be used to briefly record what was discussed along with any decisions and actions.

Record of supervision meeting			
Date			
Supervisee Name			
Supervisor Name			
Discussion focus	**Actions agreed**	**By whom**	**By when**
Issues carried forward from last supervision session – does the Supervisee feel their needs were met?			
Issues specifically noted for this session in the agenda circulated prior to the meeting			
Support for specific worries or observations raised by the Supervisee			
Reflection on progress within the setting and professional learning			
Professional development planning and training needs identified			
Issues to be carried forward to the next meeting			
Record of any areas of dissent			
A positive I am taking away from the Supervision session			
Supervisee Signature:		Date:	
Supervisor Signature:		Date:	

Appendix 5 Sample Recruitment Policy Template

Sample Recruitment Template (Barnardos)

1 RATIONALE AND POLICY CONSIDERATIONS

The Recruitment Policy in relation to an Early Years Service means a policy specifying the procedure to be followed by the registered provider when hiring employees and unpaid workers, including the steps to be taken to check and verify references, qualifications and vetting documentation.

The goals of this policy are:

* To recruit the best possible people to [*name of service*] and provide clear guidelines to management and employees on the recruitment and selection process.

* To ensure, through the recruitment and selection process, that children are protected and [*name of service*] fulfils its duty of care relating to safe recruitment and selection practice.

* To ensure the process is managed fairly without either direct or indirect discrimination towards any individual or group.

* To ensure that [*name of service*] is compliant with all relevant legislation and quality practice in this area.

LEGISLATION AND REGULATORY REQUIREMENTS

* Under Regulation 9 of the Child Care Act 1991 (Early Years Services) Regulations 2016, the registered provider must ensure that an effective management structure is in place, and appropriate people are recruited to ensure the quality and safety of the care provided to the children attending the service.

* Having a clear, written policy and procedure on recruitment is a requirement under Regulation 10 of the Child Care Act 1991 (Early Years Services) Regulations 2016. The policy must cover both paid and unpaid workers.

* Child Care Act 1991 (Early Years Services) (Amendment) Regulations 2016

* Data Protection Act 2018.

CHILDREN'S NEEDS

Children need:

* To be cared for and educated by adults who are appropriately qualified.

* The adults who care for them and provide for their education to have the attributes, knowledge, skills and competencies to provide their curriculum/ programmes of activities and meet their wellbeing, learning and development needs safely, responsibly and according to the highest quality standards.

* To be safe when in the company of adults in the setting who are there to assist their main educators (such as contractors, volunteers and students).

PARENTS'/FAMILIES' NEEDS

Parents/guardians need to:

* Be assured that the service's approach to recruiting and selecting the early years educators and other staff members who will be responsible for planning and providing for their child's care and education, while in the early years setting is professional, fair and safe.

* Know that their young child will be safe in the company of any other workers who will spend time interacting with them while they are in the service, either paid or unpaid.

STAFF NEEDS

All staff members need to know:

* That the service's recruitment and selection processes are fair, open and transparent and are not discriminatory.

* How the service recruits staff.

MANAGEMENT NEEDS

Management needs to:

* Know that the recruitment and selection process is clear and transparent for all stakeholders.

* Know that they have established safe and appropriate systems and procedures to ensure that the best possible people are recruited to the staff team to ensure the provision of a safe and good quality service.

* Ensure that they fulfil their duty of care to all stakeholders, especially the children in their care, and that all relevant legislation and regulations are fully complied with.

NATIONAL QUALITY FRAMEWORKS

* Tusla: Quality Regulatory Framework
* Síolta: The National Quality Framework for Early Childhood Education

DEFINITIONS/GLOSSARY

(Include definitions here of any words or phrases that may need explanation.)

Employee in an early years service	A person who enters into or works under a contract of employment with the registered provider
Unpaid worker in an early years service	A person who works in the service but who is not remunerated for such work by the registered provider
Verify	A process to check or prove the legality or accuracy of a document

2 POLICY STATEMENT

(Outlines the principles, values and purpose of the policy. It will generally be quite short.)

All recruitment, selection and promotion carried out in this service is in compliance with employment and equality legislation, and is informed by quality evidence-based human resource practices. The aim is always to ensure the selection of the best candidate possible for whichever post is to be filled.

All processes are fair and transparent and all appointments are made on merit and in an open and accountable manner.

All necessary steps are taken to ensure that children are protected, as far as possible, in the recruitment and selection processes, and that [name of service] fulfils its duty of care in relation to the safe recruitment and selection of all those who will have access to the children. This includes requiring appropriate Garda/police vetting and written references in accordance with Children First.

Successful recruitment depends on finding people with the necessary skills, attributes, experience and appropriately recognised qualifications (based on DCYA Early Years Recognised Qualifications) to carry out their roles competently, and the ability to make a positive contribution to upholding the service's operating principles and values and meeting its goals.

EQUAL OPPORTUNITIES

Selection of applicants is based on the applicants having the relevant qualifications, skills, competencies and experience to meet the requirements of the post, without bias on grounds of gender, marital or family status, age, disability, religion, sexual orientation, race or membership of the Traveller community (Employment Equality Acts 1998 and 2004).

Positions are open to all suitably qualified applicants who satisfy the educational and experience selection criteria relevant to each specific post. Applicants who meet the selection criteria have equal access to the selection process.

GARDA/POLICE VETTING

The Registered Owner/All Management Committee Members and Directors, the Manager and all employees of this service will each have two references taken up and will also be appropriately Garda/police vetted. Garda vetting is renewed every three years.

All other persons who work in the service such as contractors, students and volunteers will be appropriately vetted to ensure that children are protected at all times. Parents/guardians who go on occasional outings and/or who work in a supportive role with the service are not required to be vetted as they will not have unsupervised access to children other than their own.
(See Appendix 5A for guidance on essential competencies of early years care and education staff.)

3 PROCEDURES AND PRACTICES

(Outlines the specific steps and/or guidance to be followed in order to implement the policy.)

(See Appendix 5B for a sample recruitment schedule.)

JOB DESCRIPTION

All posts must have:

* A standard job description (see information in Appendix 5C) outlining the functions and objectives of the role, responsibilities and expectations, and minimum qualifications;

* A person specification of desirable attributes, skills and competencies associated with the job; and

* Details of terms and conditions of employment.

(Appendix 5D outlines sample occupational profiles.)

ADVERTISING

Recruitment advertisements will contain nothing of a discriminatory nature and will aim to encourage applications from the broadest possible base. They will comply with all relevant legislation including the Equal Status legislation.

THE APPLICATION PROCESS

All applicants must be given a comprehensive job description, person specification, information on the terms and conditions of employment, a Garda vetting form and appropriate background information on the post, at application stage.

All candidates will be required to submit a fully completed standard application form **or** an up-to-date curriculum vitae detailing their education, training and employment history. (The advertisement for the post will specify which is required.)

Any identified gaps in an applicant's education/ training/employment history will be investigated.

False or misleading information given on the application, Garda vetting form or medical form may be considered a breach of trust and may lead to non-appointment, disciplinary procedures or may prevent the employee being confirmed in post.

SHORTLISTING FOR INTERVIEW

Candidates are selected for interview based on the objective requirements of the post and those with relevant qualifications and experience at the level of the post, based on the job description and person specification, will normally be selected for interview.

All applicants are screened and replied to within [*specify a reasonable timeframe*]. Candidates who clearly best meet the requirements of the position, based on their application, are brought forward to the next stage of the recruitment process.

Should the number of applicants who meet the basic requirements of the post be too large to interview all the candidates, further shortlisting may be required giving preference to those candidates who, on the basis of the quality of their application, are most likely to succeed at interview stage.

METHODS OF ASSESSMENT

All those who apply for a position are assessed on the following:

1. Application form/curriculum vitae
2. Interview (see Appendix 5E for a sample interview process and Appendix 5F for a sample interview scoresheet)
3. Satisfactory identity confirmation
4. Satisfactory reference checks

5. Qualifications

6. Satisfactory Garda/police vetting

1. Application form/curriculum vitae

Application forms/CVs are assessed at the shortlisting stage to determine whether the applicant meets the essential requirements for the position. The quality of the application may also form part of this assessment.

2. Interview

Prior to interviews, an interview panel is convened to agree the interview format and core areas of questioning. This panel normally comprises three people (always a minimum of two people) with at least one external. A competency-based, weighted marking scheme in line with the job description and person specification will be drafted and agreed.

A member of the interview board who has a personal or professional relationship to an applicant must declare that relationship to other members of the board and a decision will be taken by the *registered provider/owner/committee* as to whether their participation as an interviewer is appropriate.

Candidates invited for interview are informed of the time, date and venue for interview in writing as early as possible.

Before the interview is completed the candidate is informed of the next step in the process.

The shortlisted candidate from the interview process is informed of [*name of service*]'s interest but also informed that a formal offer will only be made when satisfactory reference and Garda/police vetting information are obtained.

All candidates are informed of the outcome in writing within [*specify a reasonable timeframe*].

3. Confirmation of identity

Prior to an appointee taking up any post their identity must be confirmed against some statutory documentation (such as a passport, driver's licence, public services card or ID card), which gives their full name, address, signature and photograph. A copy of the ID will be kept on file.

4. Reference checks

An applicant must submit names of two referees who will be contacted by [*name of person responsible*] in confidence, one of whom must be a current employer if the person is employed or the most recent employer if not.

Where the applicant has been employed in the early years sector, a reference will be sought where practicable.

In the case of internal applicants who have been employed in this service for five years or more, [*name of registered provider*], the registered provider of this service, as their employer, can provide a reference.

Where a reference from a previous employer is not available, references will be sought from another reputable person or persons (a highly regarded, well thought of, respected person who is independent, unbiased and not a family member.) Character references will not be obtained instead of appropriate employer references.

It is the responsibility of [*name of person responsible on behalf of the registered provider*] to check references and to ensure that they are satisfied as to the character and suitability and relevant experience of the candidate **prior** to any person being appointed or allowed access to a child in the service.

All referees must be contacted in person/by phone in order to:

* Either obtain an oral reference, which must be documented on an oral reference form, signed and dated by [*name*] and recorded confidentially on the employee's file; or

* Verify a written reference from the referee. The referee is asked to confirm that they wrote the reference. The reference, once verified, is signed and dated by the registered provider or the named person responsible on behalf of the registered provider [*name*].

References will only be obtained from a current employer with the candidate's permission and after all other references have been taken up.

Board members and directors of the board are required to have two written, validated references.

5. Qualifications

Each person appointed to work directly with children must either hold the appropriate minimum qualifications for the post or a confirmed exemption under the Grandfathering Clause or the Access and Inclusion Model (AIM).

[*Include an appendix giving appropriate minimum qualifications and exemptions, which can be found at* www.dcya.gov.ie/documents/earlyyears/20171018DCYAEarlyYears RecognisedQualifications.pdf. *Refer to this appendix here.*]

Qualifications are verified by viewing the original certificate, a certified copy of the certificate, the original transcript or certified copy of the transcript. [*The registered provider*] will document that the appropriate document has been verified. [*See the explanatory notes in* Tusla's Quality and Regulatory Framework *for further information on 'certified copy'.*]

6. Garda vetting

All applicants must submit a properly completed Garda vetting form when an offer of position has been made.

Police vetting must be submitted when an offer of a position has been made and where a person has worked in a state or country outside of Ireland for six consecutive months where it is practicable to do so.

[*Name of service*] reserves the right not to appoint an applicant if any unacceptable* previous criminal conviction/s record, prosecution/s (successful or not, pending or completed), or a query related to their identity comes to light and/or was not disclosed at application stage.

[**You might consider including the following in this section also:* The management reserves the right to decide whether the information on the Garda vetting disclosure makes the record 'unacceptable' having considered all the circumstances and the available information.]

[*If you have a Records and Record Keeping Policy and/or a Confidentiality Policy, refer to them here.*]

[Note: Assessing a disclosure:

If you find someone has a criminal record it doesn't automatically mean they will be unsuitable.

You need to consider:

* The nature of the offence
* How long ago it took place
* Its relevance to the job
* The risk to children if it were to be repeated.

Motoring offences, for example, may not need to be a prohibition to an offer of employment unless the job involves driving the children.

Where a vetting disclosure is received which causes concern regarding a candidate, the service must undertake a comprehensive risk assessment to determine the suitability of the candidate for employment.]

[*If the service is a community service and recruits staff through the Community Employment Childcare Training and Development Programme, include the following paragraph here:*

It is essential that all adults who work with the children in the service are suitable, therefore those who are recruited through employment schemes such as the Community Employment Childcare Training and Development Programme (CE) are required to undergo a thorough selection and assessment process in the same way as other employees.]

Further important detailed information from Tusla on qualifications, references and Garda/Police Vetting is included in Regulation 9 of Tusla's Quality and Regulatory Framework.

CANVASSING

Canvassing – that is, making an approach to secure advantage – is an unacceptable practice and may lead to disqualification. However, it is entirely reasonable for a candidate to seek information about [*name of service*]. This contact is not part of the interview process and candidates will not be advantaged or disadvantaged by such contact.

FOLLOWING SELECTION

All employees will be given a written statement of their terms and conditions of employment on application where possible and at least within **two months** of commencement of employment.

All employees are given an information pack and a copy of the Staff Handbook on commencement of employment.

PROBATION

All new employees are on probation for the first twelve months of employment.

A review of the employee's performance must take place with the employee halfway through the probation period and again at the end of the probation period. The manager must set standards and goals and the candidate must be clear on the service's expectations.

[*Name of service*] (the employer) reserves the right to extend the probation period if appropriate or terminate employment during this period should the employee prove unsuitable for the post. Probation periods may be extended to compensate for extended absences during the probation period.

No employee will be confirmed in post until the [*registered provider/management committee*] receives a satisfactory report in writing [*from the manager*] on their performance at the end of the probation period. The employee will be informed in writing as to the outcome at the end of the probation period.

INDUCTION, SUPERVISION, SUPPORT AND TRAINING DURING PROBATION PERIOD (SEE STAFF TRAINING POLICY)

All new employees must be given induction training on commencement of employment with [*name of service*]. The employee is required to sign the induction checklist confirming they are happy that all areas listed were appropriately covered.

During the induction period, new staff members will be required to familiarise themselves with all the service's policies, procedures and statements. All staff members will receive regular support and supervision to enable them to perform their role effectively.

CONTRACTS OF SERVICE

Careful consideration must be given to the type of contract offered to prospective employees.

[*State here that a written contract will be issued appropriate to the position.*]

CONTRACT OF EMPLOYMENT

The contract of employment will include the following:

* The employee's name, address and telephone number.

* Their date of birth, and photographic proof of identity confirming that they are over 18 years of age.

* The name and telephone number of the employee's next of kin to be notified in an emergency.

* The date of commencement in the service.

* The job description, to include role and responsibility.

* Terms and conditions of employment.

RECORD-KEEPING

* A Personnel Records file must be opened and maintained for each employee of [*name of service*] (Organisation of Working Time Act 1997). Staff members may have access to their own personnel files.

* [*Name of service*] will keep:
  — References, Garda vetting and police vetting for a period of five years after the person starts working in the service. This includes current staff and staff who are no longer working in the service
  — All other records on ex-employees for at least three years. After three years the files are reduced and only essential information is retained in accordance with GDPR requirements.

* Paperwork on candidates who were unsuccessful at interview is kept in accordance with GDPR requirements.

* Personnel records are stored in a confidential folder at [*state where*] in accordance with GDPR requirements.

* All confidential personnel information is disposed of safely by [*the registered provider/manager*] following required retention periods, by shredding.

4 COMMUNICATION PLAN

(For staff and families)

A copy of this Policy and Procedures and its Appendices will be available during all hours of operation to all staff team members and parents in the Policy Folder located in _____.

Parents/guardians may receive a copy of the policy at any time upon request.

Parents/guardians and staff members will receive written notification of any updates.

5 RELATED POLICIES, PROCEDURES AND FORMS

(List of all related documents. The policies in bold are those required under the Early Years Regulations 2016.)

* **Inclusion Policy**
* Induction Policy and Procedures
* Child Protection Policy and Procedures
* Confidentiality Policy
* Record Keeping Policy
* Garda Vetting Form
* Application Form

5 REFERENCES/SUPPORTING DOCUMENTS/ RELATED LEGISLATION

(List any relevant legislation and practice guides referred to in drafting the policy.)

* Tusla: Quality Regulatory Framework
* Child Care Act 1991
* Child Care Act 1991 (Early Years Services) Regulations 2016 and Child Care Act 1991 (Early Years Services) (Amendment) Regulations 2016
* Registrations, Early Years Inspectorate, Tusla
* *Our Duty to Care: The Principles of Good Practice for the Protection of Children and Young People*
* National Vetting Bureau, An Garda Síochana

* NPCC: ACRO Criminal Records Office, International Child Protection Certificate (UK)

* UK Government, Disclosure and Barring Service

* Barnardos Vetting Service

* Early Childhood Ireland Garda Vetting

* Equal Status (Amendment) Act 2012

* DCYA, Early Years Recognised Qualifications

* National Vetting Bureau (Children and Vulnerable Persons) Act 2012

* DCYA: Diversity, Equality and Inclusion Charter and Guidelines for Early Childhood Care and Education

* Children First Act 2015

* NERA: National Employment Rights Agency

* *Recruitment and Retention: A Good Practice Guide for Early Years, Childcare and Playwork Providers* (Sure Start, DfES 2003)

6 WHO MUST OBSERVE THIS POLICY

This policy must be observed by all registered providers, managers and all staff members.

Actions to be taken if the policy is not implemented:

(Add any relevant actions to be taken)

8 CONTACT INFORMATION

If you need more information about this policy, contact:

Name: _____

Phone number: _____

Email: _____

Policy created on [*date*] _____.

Approved by:

Name: _____

Position: _____

Signature: _____

Date this policy will be reviewed: _____

APPENDIX 5A ESSENTIAL COMPETENCIES OF EARLY YEARS CARE AND EDUCATION STAFF

A crucial element in providing quality early years care and education services is the knowledge, skills and competencies of the staff team members.

The quality of the early years care and education service and the programme is directly linked to the skills and competencies of the staff members.

(Provide a list of the essential professional competencies for early years care and education staff. The following are useful sources of information for this:

* Skills and Competencies Framework for Early Years Professionals (Crann & NCN 2016)

* CORE, Competence Requirements in Early Childhood Education and Care (European Commission 2011)

APPENDIX 5B SAMPLE RECRUITMENT SCHEDULE

Task	Approximate duration of task	Example of schedule with dates: Start date 1 September 2022
Draft job descriptions and person specification	One week	8 September 2022
Draft advertisement		10 September 2022
Decide which publication and/or website to advertise in and confirm price		14 September 2022
Advert placed in paper and/or website		17 September 2022
Include deadline for receipt of applications in advert	Three weeks from publication of advert	7 October 2022
Photocopy applications and send to shortlisting panel	One week	14 October 2022
Shortlisting	One week	21 October 2022
Interview invitation letters sent out	Two weeks' notice required to candidates	5 November 2022
Interviews	One day	8 November 2022

Task	Approximate duration of task	Example of schedule with dates: Start date 1 September 2022
Informing all candidates of interview outcome	Half a day	10 November 2022
Selected candidate – Garda vetting, check references, etc.	One month to allow for Garda vetting	10 December 2022
Appointment	Candidate may need to give notice to previous employer (this could be up to one month), which will determine start date in new position	10 December 2022
Inform other candidates that they have been unsuccessful/placed on a panel		10 December 2022

APPENDIX 5C JOB DESCRIPTIONS

(Standard job descriptions outlining the functions and objectives of the various roles in your service along with responsibilities and expectations, and minimum qualifications)

APPENDIX 5D OCCUPATIONAL PROFILES

(Occupational profiles for the various roles in your service)

APPENDIX 5E SAMPLE EARLY YEARS CARE AND EDUCATION ASSISTANT INTERVIEW PROCESS

Date of interviews: _____

Panel:

Name: _____

Name: _____

Name: _____

The three priority competency areas are as follows:

For example:

1. Suitability to work with young children

2. Appropriate qualifications to implement the early years programme

3. Ability to work as a team member under direct supervision with appropriate effectiveness and respect

Chairperson of the panel: _____

Introduce the panel.

Ensure candidate:

* Has received all relevant information

* Understands the nature of the job and the conditions of employment

* Understands how the interview will run (first general questions, then team performance questions, then practice questions, then closing)

* Understands the process of decision-making thereafter.

General questions: [*Name of panel member who will ask these questions*]

* Include general questions here

Team performance: [*Name panel member*]

* Include questions relating to team performance here

Practice: [*Name panel member*]

* Include questions related to early years care and education practice here

Chairperson:

* Are there any questions you would like to ask us or anything you would like to say that you did not have the opportunity to say earlier?

Summary

When you will notify them of outcome

Thank you and goodbye

APPENDIX 5F EARLY YEARS CARE AND EDUCATION ASSISTANT – INTERVIEW SCORE SHEET

(Information on the method of scoring you will use when interviewing job candidates)

APPENDIX 5G GARDA/POLICE VETTING REQUIREMENTS

(Details of Garda/police vetting requirements for employees, boards of management and directors and students (including Transition Year students). This information is available in Tusla's Quality and Regulatory Framework.)

Appendix 6 Tusla Early Years Inspectorate CAPA Form

CORRECTIVE AND PREVENTIVE ACTIONS (CAPA) TO ADDRESS NON-COMPLIANCES

SECTION A

DCYA Number:	
Tusla Identifier No:	
Name of Service:	
Service Address line 1:	
Service Address line 2:	
Service Address line 3:	
Date of Last Inspection:	
Date of CAPA Issue:	

SECTION B

Corrective and Preventive Actions (CAPA)

Regulation Number	Corrective and Preventive Actions (Using the SMART rule: Specific, Measurable, Achievable, Realistic and Timely)	Timeframe	For office use only EYI comments
	Corrective Action		
	Preventive Action		

Regulation Number	Corrective and Preventive Actions	Timeframe	For office use only EYI comments
	Corrective Action		
	Preventive Action		
Regulation Number	Corrective and Preventive Actions	Timeframe	For office use only EYI comments
	Corrective Action		
	Preventive Action		
Regulation Number	Corrective and Preventive Actions	Timeframe	For office use only EYI comments
	Corrective Action		
	Preventive Action		
Regulation Number	Corrective and Preventive Actions	Timeframe	For office use only EYI comments
	Corrective Action		
	Preventive Action		

Regulation Number	Corrective and Preventive Actions	Timeframe	For office use only EYI comments
	Corrective Action		
	Preventive Action		

CAPA submitted by Registered Provider*: *or person authorised by the Registered Provider	Document name	Date of submission

SECTION C FOR TUSLA INTERNAL OFFICE USE ONLY

Corrective Actions and Preventive Actions (CAPA) reviewed on date: ___/___/___

Reviewed by:

Timeframe	Name and Title

Outcome:

Are the Corrective and Preventive Actions addressing the non-compliances?
Yes ☐ No ☐

If No, insert date of request for revised Corrective and Preventive
Action Form: __ /__ /__

Note: One additional opportunity to submit CAPA only as per the Early Years
Inspectorate (EYI) Development and Approval of Inspection Reports Procedure.

Resubmitted Corrective and Preventive Form

Updated Corrective Actions and Preventive Actions (CAPA) received on date: __ /__ /__

Updated Corrective Actions and Preventive Actions (CAPA) reviewed on date: __ /__ /__

Reviewed by:

Timeframe	Name and Title

Outcome:

Are the Resubmitted Provided Corrective and Preventive Actions addressing the non- compliances? Yes ☐ No ☐

If No, document date escalated to Registration Panel: _____

Signed and dated (Lead Inspector)

Name	Title

Index